"My friend, Dennis Lee, is a S... get a chance to hang out with a theologian, it's either going to be the most fascinating or most boring afternoon of your life. The difference will be in how cautiously and practically he or she can break down the concepts being discussed. Dennis is that practical theologian, who makes very deep and profound Biblical concepts easily understood. You will find this reflected in the way he writes. This is a very encouraging book!"

- Randy Greer,
Senior Pastor Trinity Life Center,
Assembly of God, Las Vegas, NV.

"From Here to There: A Journey to Spiritual Transformation", written by Pastor Dennis Lee, is a book that I would define as a roadmap to promise and a guidebook to significant fulfillment in Christ. Through extensive research and reliance upon God's Word, Dennis has prepared a "pathway" of practical steps and sure-footedness that, if followed, will certainly lead to a remarkable freedom and a fresh knowledge of living in God's presence. This work clearly echoes the wisdom of Proverbs 3:6: "In all your ways acknowledge Him, and He shall direct your paths."

- Glenn C. Burris,
Jr., President,
The Foursquare Church.

"Whether young or old, we can identify areas in our lives that limit and hinder us from being who God has called us to be. We want to grow and to change, but in the complexity of our world, knowing what to do can seem overwhelming and confusing. "From Here to There" uses the timeless truths of God's Word to show a simple pathway to personal transformation. I believe that those who read this book will recommend it to others."

- Kimberly Dirmann,
Southwest District Supervisor,
The Foursquare Church.

"Dennis has written a book that will be used to reach the lost, as well as being an excellent resource for developing disciples; I especially liked his stories in relating to biblical truth.

I believe that Dennis hit the mark in writing a book that demonstrates how following God's Word, the Bible, can help anyone discover how to remake his or her life. This book is well researched and is based on the best material available today, the Bible. I look forward to sharing this book with my team and using it to grow disciples in God's Kingdom."

- Bill J. Stevenson,
Senior Pastor,
First Baptist Church, Mesquite, NV.

From Here to There

A Journey To Spiritual Transformation

Written by
Dennis Lee

Edited by
Mike Donahue

Copyright © 2015 by Dennis Lee

From Here to There
A Journey To Spiritual Transformation
by Dennis Lee

Printed in the United States of America.

ISBN 9781498442992

All rights reserved solely by the author. The author guarantees all contents are original and do not infringe upon the legal rights of any other person or work. No part of this book may be reproduced in any form without the permission of the author. The views expressed in this book are not necessarily those of the publisher.

Unless otherwise indicated, Scripture quotations are taken from the New King James Version (NKJV). Copyright © 1979, 1980, 1982 by Thomas Nelson, Inc. Used by permission. All rights reserved.

www.xulonpress.com

Spiritual Formation Series

Spiritual formation is probably the most important process undertaken by a Christian. The goal is to grow into the likeness of Jesus Christ. It's about actively engaging with God and His Word, the Bible, following its commands in and through the power of the Holy Spirit.

The Bible tells us not to be conformed to or by any worldly standards, but rather we are to be transformed, that is, a change that happens within through the renewing of our minds and hearts, Romans 12:2, because as a person thinks in their hearts, that is who they will become, Proverbs 23:7.

The Apostle Peter says it's all about growing in both the grace and knowledge of our Savior and Lord, Jesus Christ, 2 Peter 3:18.

Pastor Dennis Lee is writing a series of books dealing with discipleship and doctrine to help the reader grow, not only in their knowledge of God, but also in how to apply biblical reality to everyday life.

The series includes:
"From Here to There: A Journey to Spiritual Transformation"
"Wells of Living Waters" (Coming Soon)
"A Layman's Guide to Biblical Doctrine"(Coming 2016)
"A Spiritual First Aid Manual" (Coming 2017)

TABLE OF CONTENTS

Introduction xi

1. The Road You Take Matters 17
2. Who Are You? 27
3. Scrubbed And Cleansed 40
4. Aligning With God and His Word 51
5. Aligning With God's Will and Way 60
6. The Process of Alignment 77
7. Filled and Overflowing 90
8. Surrendered and Submitted 102
9. Agents of Change 115
10. Being and Staying On-Purpose 128
11. Pursuing God's Presence 141
12. Potholes that Damage Transformation 153
13. God's Speed Bumps 166
14. Maintaining Your Gains 178

Introduction

Bookstore shelves are lined with volumes and the Internet is loaded with sites offering readers transformational change. There are a multitude of philosophies promising solutions to the multifaceted complexities faced by humanity. People are looking for something that works; something that can help them remake their lives.

Most of the available philosophies of life and change, however, are more about the fad flavor of the day. In the long run they are lacking and have come up short. They have proven unreliable as true agents of change. What's being sold isn't working. How else can we explain the ever-growing and record-setting number of divorces, rapes, and suicides, as well as the high levels of abuse, addiction and depression, not to mention any number of deviant behaviors?

I have found getting back to the basics can help us find answers to life's spiritual questions. We need to return to God's Word, the Bible, God's instructions on how to live in this crazy mixed up world.

"From Here to There: A Journey To Spiritual Transformation" is filled with timeless biblical principles that work for real spiritual transformation. This book doesn't reinvent these principles, it revitalizes, rejuvenates, and restores them within a person's life, allowing each of us to reach spiritual goals, and get heavenly results. This book isn't about success stories from other people. It demonstrates how following God's Word can help us discover our own paths and create our own stories of success.

What you need to ask

Are you where you want to be? Can you say right here and now without hesitation you are where you want to be in your relationship with God? Are you satisfied in that relationship?

If you are truthful, the answer is probably a painful "No." Solomon, who had the wisdom of God at his disposal, answered the same way.

"There is not a righteous man on earth who does what is right and never sins." (Ecclesiastes 7:20 New International Version, or NIV)

Even the great spiritual giants of the Old and New Testaments knew this to be true. The prophet Isaiah cried out to the Lord:

"Woe is me, for I am undone! Because I am a man of unclean lips and I dwell in the midst of a people of unclean lips; for my eyes have seen the King, the Lord of hosts." (Isaiah 6:5)

The Apostle Paul, a champion and missionary for Jesus Christ, set up churches throughout Asia, Greece, and Italy, and recognized he wasn't always where he should have been spiritually.

"The very things I want to do, I don't, and the things I don't want to do, those are the things that I do." (Romans 7:15)

We all need to grow in our relationship with God. This requires spiritual transformation; a transformation we experience daily. Change is a journey, not a destination. The end of this journey is when we stand before God in heaven. It is a destination toward which we are constantly moving while still on this side of eternity, while we are still on this earth.

Jesus encouraged those who wanted to accompany Him on this journey.

"If anyone desires to come after Me, let him deny himself, and take up his cross daily, and follow Me." (Luke 9:23)

Introduction

As you read this book and travel the journey toward spiritual transformation and a closer relationship with God, record your findings and feelings. Note what you need to do in order to further your relationship with the Lord as He reveals it to you, and then how you will accomplish it.

Follow the Yellow Brick Road

Our spiritual journey is analogous to Dorothy's journey in the "Wizard of Oz" by Frank Baum.

In the book, Dorothy and her dog Toto are transported to the Land of Oz by a tornado that rips through her family's farm in Kansas. The twister picks up the farmhouse in which Dorothy and Toto are hiding and plops it down in Munchkin Land in Oz. To get back to Kansas, Dorothy is advised by the munchkins to travel the Yellow Brick Road to the Emerald City where the Wizard of Oz will surely help her.

Dorothy takes the road and along the way to the Emerald City meets some strange characters including the Scarecrow, Tin Man, and Cowardly Lion. The three decide to accompany Dorothy to see if the Wizard might endow them with qualities each believe they lack; brains for the Scarecrow, a heart for the Tin Man, and courage for the Lion. Throughout the perilous journey on the Yellow Brick Road, the Wicked Witch of the West harasses the trio.

The journey we're on from this world to God's heavenly home, we need what the three characters with Dorothy discovered within themselves: the Scarecrow's wisdom, the Tin Man's love and compassion, and the Lion's courage. We need these characteristics because we constantly face and battle with Satan, our own Wicked Witch of the West.

How to use "From Here to There: A Journey to Spiritual Transformation"

Over the years I have found myself quickly breezing through different books. I'd have a chapter finished in an hour or so and within the week the book would be done and then it was off to another book. The problem with reading like this is that too often whatever's read is soon forgotten or placed in a holding pattern while new material is being consumed.

This is no way to embrace and retain material, and the lessons it may be teaching. It takes a person 90 days to change a habit. To allow the spiritual transformation taught in this book to take root, don't race through it and quickly move onto something else. Read it slowly and write down what the Lord is saying specifically to you.

For maximum retention and effectiveness, record the actions you need to take and what changes are necessary to be everything God has designed and created for you. Keep a calendar to see how you're progressing. At the end of each chapter there are questions for either personal reflection or group discussion. Please take the necessary time to answer these and see what the Lord may be saying to you through them. Take time to review them and ponder their implications applying the steps God has revealed.

Finally take time to review this book and your devotional journey every year to make sure you are moving in the direction of true spiritual transformation.

My source of inspiration

Throughout my years as a pastor I have read, studied, and presented hundreds of sermons and teachings. Much of the material in this book isn't new but is based on what I have learned over 36 years of being seminary trained, a senior pastor and teacher, and living as a Christian. Some of this material is unique to this book, while some

Introduction

has been presented in different ways by multiple authors and in various forms.

The material in "From Here to There: A Journey to Spiritual Transformation" was supplied by the Holy Spirit over the past two years and has been living and growing inside me. It has only recently been set down in this format and is based on a sermon series I taught throughout 2013. The material in this book can be used by anyone without worry of any infringement, as Jesus told His disciples.

"Freely you have received, freely give." (Matthew 10:8)

I hope this material can be used to help as many as possible in their journey toward spiritual transformation.

CHAPTER ONE

THE ROAD YOU TAKE MATTERS

In Lewis Carroll's "Alice's Adventures in Wonderland," Alice comes to a fork in the road and is unsure which way to go. Talking to herself and pondering her options, Alice hears a voice singing. It's the Cheshire Cat staring down at her from his perch in a tree.

"Which way should I go?" Alice asks the cat.
"Well, that depends on where you want to get to," the cat replies.
"It really doesn't matter," Alice says.
"Then it really doesn't matter which way you go," says the cat.[1]

But it really does matter which way you go.

The chorus of John Denver's song "Country Road" goes, "Country Road take me home to the place I belong, West Virginia, Mountain Mama, take me home, country road."

For me, the place I want to go isn't West Virginia no matter if it is almost heaven or what Mountain Mama says. The place I want to go is heaven.

It's good to know our destination, especially when eternity is at stake. It's imperative we sit down before our journey, look at a map or GPS app, and decide which way is best. It's foolish not to. We could end

---

[1] Alice in Wonderland, directed by Clyde Geronimi Director (1951, Burbank, CA: Walt Disney Pictures, 2000), DVD

up in a city and a destination never intended. We therefore must have an end in mind or we'll travel around aimlessly.

In the biblical text, Jesus talks about two ways for someone to get to their eternal destination. Gates provide access to both. Jesus gives us a warning to make sure we choose the right one.

"Enter by the narrow gate, for wide is the gate and broad is the way that leads to destruction, and there are many who go in by it. Because narrow is the gate and difficult is the way which leads to life, and there are few who find it." (Matthew 7:13-14)

In ancient times impressive walls surrounded cities. They were designed to keep the enemy out. The only way in or out was through one of the city's gates. Some of the gates were wide enough to allow many people, animals, and equipment to pass through at the same time. Others were quite narrow, permitting only one person at a time. As one might imagine very few people chose the small narrow gates.

On a trip to Jerusalem, our guide took us through one of these narrow gates in the old city. It was a small opening where you stepped over the threshold while ducking at the same time. At the point where I started to step over the threshold, a noise caused me to look back. When I turned back to enter, I forgot to duck and banged my head sharply against the lintel above the door. I almost passed out. I'll never forget that narrow gate experience.

It is just such a small, narrow gate that Jesus describes leading to the road of eternal life. He says this gate is small, the way narrow, and there are few who will find it and enter.

Highway to hell

The wide gate and the road to which it leads is the more popular route because its broad width allows a multitude of opinions and beliefs. In reality it's the "Highway to Hell."

People who choose this path often say things like, "All roads lead to God," believing a person can be a Buddhist, Hindu, Jehovah's Witness, Jewish, Mormon, Muslim, Scientologist, a Christian Scientist, New Ager, or whatever, and still get to heaven. They believe all religions are paths to God and God will accept everyone who is religious in any way, shape, or form. This also extends to those with no particular belief system or who believe in everything and a whole lot of nothing.

The only problem with this sort of thinking is that it makes Jesus a liar, because Jesus said He is the only way.

"I am the way, the truth, and the life. No one comes to the Father except through Me." (John 14:6)

People who choose the wide way also say, "All that's matters is that I'm sincere."

While they may be sincere, they may also be sincerely wrong. A person may sincerely believe the law of gravity no longer applies or doesn't exist, but if they jump off a building they soon discover all their positive sincerity didn't do one ounce of good; they fall despite their beliefs.

But the pièce de résistance that sends more people down this Highway to Hell is, "God wouldn't really send anyone to hell." This belief is based on a lack of knowledge about God and who He is. God doesn't send anyone to hell, we send ourselves. We're the ones who enter by the wide gate and travel on the wide way instead of the way God gave us through Jesus Christ, the narrow gate.

"For God so loved the world that He gave His only begotten Son, that whoever believes in Him should not perish but have everlasting life. For God did not send His Son into the world to condemn the world but that the world through Him might be saved." (John 3:16-17)

The wide gate and road is the way of the world. There are no hindrances or resistances upon entering the wide gate because it comes naturally to humanity. We enter the wide gate without even thinking because it takes absolutely no thought whatsoever. It's attractive to the senses and it simply seems like "the thing to do." It's where everyone is going. It's where the action is!

The way is wide open and easy to travel, much like our interstate highways. We can travel fast and get where we want to go with relative ease. We are also enticed by the many billboards telling us we can make a quick exit, partake in our pleasure with no accountability, and then get right back on the highway with ease. This is a picture of our current world system with all its enticements and temptations that are so easily accessible.

The only difficulty about the wide way is it eventually comes to an end. Those who travel it rarely, if ever, pay attention to this reality. There are so many things that capture a person's attention they seldom have time to consider where this road is actually leading, which is a cliff and everlasting torment.

Travelers on the wide way desire the crowds and the attractions it provides. They are willing to run the risk of wrecking their lives with everyone else. The great tragedy is they ignore the warning signs along the way, never preparing to face the abyss below.

"There is a way that seems right to a man, but its end is the way of death." (Proverbs 14:12)

There is another way, a better way, however.

The narrow way to heaven

The narrow way is the way less traveled. It is often referred to as the "Highway to Heaven," but this is a misnomer since it isn't wide at all. The reason it isn't wide and traveled more is because the gate is narrow. Travel on the narrow way comes only through faith in Jesus Christ, because the gate is only one person wide and that person is Jesus, who explains:

"I am the gate. Whoever enters through me will be saved. He will come in and go out, and find pasture." (John 10:9 NIV)

"I am the way, the truth, and the life. No one comes to the Father except through Me." (John 14:6)

Jesus is not one of many ways to get to Heaven. He is the only way.

This Biblical truth is also recorded in the book of Acts.

"Salvation is found in no one else, for there is no other name under heaven given to men by which we must be saved." (Acts 4:12)

In fact, the gate is so narrow it cannot initially be seen. "… Only a few will find it." You must search for it. You must intentionally seek it. This will only happen when you get tired of traveling on the wide way and think, "There's got to be more to life than this!"

This is how it happened in my life. I was living the high life and I was well off, according to the world. I had a multi-million dollar business and all the perks that accompany it. I was a partier and would often go out drinking and drugging.

One New Years Eve I went out and got wasted. When I got home the next morning, however, I was surprisingly sober. I looked up to heaven and said, "There's got to be a better way? There's got to be more to life than this?" But then I gave a dismissive gesture saying, "Oh, You aren't listening anyway."

But God was listening and over the next several months He dried up all my connections. He also had someone share the gospel with me and invite me to a home Bible study.

It wasn't long afterward that I gave my life to Jesus Christ and my life hasn't been the same since. There have been hardships, but the Lord has always kept His promises.

During my journey I discovered the narrow way requires a driver with more precision than I have in order to stay the course. When people tell me that God is their co-pilot, I quickly tell them to switch seats.

When I think of this narrow way I think of many narrow, turbulent, backcountry roads I've driven. The narrow way Jesus talks about is similar. It is unpaved, covered with gravel, and fallen rocks. It is also filled with twists and turns, requiring an attention to detail and a determination to stay on course.

Yet, no matter how determined we may be to stay the course, sin always has a way of jumping out to trip us up.

We need someone greater than ourselves to navigate this road. That someone is Jesus. Jesus is not only the door, but the road as well. Jesus said He is the way, the truth, and the life. (John 14:6a)

In addition to being the way, Jesus is also the truth. By its very nature truth is narrow. Either something is true or it isn't. Scripture teaches that truth is truth regardless of whether we agree with it or not. Our opinion of the truth really doesn't matter. Whether we believe in the truth of gravity doesn't change its reality. It doesn't matter whether we like the truth of God's Word; it's still true.

Unlike the wide way, the narrow way doesn't end. Instead it leads to a glorious world not yet seen, but promised.

"What is seen is temporary but what is unseen is eternal." (2 Corinthians 4:18b NIV)

The path we choose to travel is our decision. We can either choose the easy, wide way, the Highway to Hell, or we can diligently seek out the more difficult narrow way that leads to heaven.

Some seek out the narrow way but never take it. They decide it's too narrow, requires too much sacrifice, and it would be too uncomfortable, so they automatically default back to the wide way. Our goal should be to finish this life well and hear the Lord's encouragement.

"Well done good and faithful servant, enter into the joy of your Lord." (Matthew 25:21, 23)

Today, decide to take the road less traveled, it will make all the difference in the world.

What you can do

How can you enter and stay on this narrow way?

1. Ask Jesus Christ to be your Savior and Lord

"Most assuredly, I say to you, unless one is born again, he cannot see the kingdom of God." (John 3:3)

"If you confess with your mouth the Lord Jesus and believe in your heart that God has raised Him from the dead, you will be saved. For with the heart one believes unto righteousness, and with the mouth confession is made unto salvation." (Romans 10:9-10)

To make this confession, take a moment to say this prayer out loud.

"Dear Lord, I confess I need you!

"I confess with my mouth and believe with my heart that Jesus is the Son of God, that Jesus died on the Cross of Calvary to free me from the bondage of sin and death.

"I confess that I am a sinner and need forgiveness. I believe there's only one way to have eternal life and enter the Kingdom of Heaven, and that's through Your Son, Jesus Christ. I believe Jesus died on the cross and on the third day rose from the dead, and that Jesus is the way, the truth, and the life, and no one comes to You except through Him.

"I ask right now that You Lord Jesus come into my life to become my personal Savior and Lord. Please fill me and baptize me with Your Holy Spirit and lead me on the path of righteousness. Be the lamp unto my feet, and the light to my path.

"I believe through this confession of faith I am Your child, a child of God. I believe my past is done away with and that I am a brand new creation created in Christ Jesus. "Amen!"

This is something we can all believe in because salvation isn't by any good works we might do, or through any particular religion we belong to. Rather it is by grace through faith that we are saved.

"For by grace you have been saved through faith, and that not of yourselves; it is the gift of God, not of works, lest anyone should boast." (Ephesians 2:8-9)

2. Be baptized

Once the people heard the good news, the gospel message, once they entered through the narrow gate and onto the narrow way, they were told by the disciples to be baptized. This is what the Apostle Peter told more than 3,000 people who came to belief in his very first sermon.

"What must we do?" they asked.

"Repent and let every one of you be baptized in the name of Jesus Christ for the remission of sins and you shall receive the gift of the Holy Spirit." (Acts 3:38; cf. Acts 2:41; 8:12; 36-38)

While the act of baptism is symbolic, it's an important first step on this narrow way that Jesus commanded of us.

"Go therefore and make disciples of all the nations, baptizing them in the name of the Father and of the Son and of the Holy Spirit, teaching them to observe all things that I have commanded you; and lo, I am with you always, even to the end of the age." (Matthew 28:19-20)

If you have come into the saving faith of Jesus Christ, contact a church pastor and ask him to baptize you in the name of the Father, Son and Holy Spirit.

3. Get connected with a local church

Find a Bible-believing, Bible-teaching church and get involved. God never called us to walk on this journey alone but with others. The writer of Hebrews instructs us to do this.

"And let us consider one another in order to stir up love and good works, not forsaking the assembling of ourselves together, as is the manner of some, but exhorting one another, and so much the more as you see the Day approaching." (Hebrews 10:24-25)

Finding a church to call home will help us on our journey. It will benefit us in ways we could never imagine. It will become an extended family. It will be a place where friendships are built and encouraged. It will help us find God's purpose and plan for life. It will help us utilize our God-given talents and ministry. It will keep us grounded in God's Word, allowing God's Word to minister into our lives.

REFLECTION AND DISCUSSION

1. Describe when you entered the "narrow gate" and accepted Jesus Christ as your Savior and Lord. (Matthew 7:13-14)

2. What excuses have you or do you still use not to accept Jesus Christ as your Savior and enter through the narrow gate?

3. What temptations continue to entice you to pull off the narrow road? What does God's Word say? (1 John 1:9)

4. How has entering by the narrow gate and traveling down the narrow road changed your life?

5. When and where were you baptized? Have you found a Bible believing church and are you connected? How?

6. What one thing will you take away from this chapter and apply to your life?

Chapter Two

Who Are You

In "Alice in Wonderland" Alice encounters the alphabet-speaking caterpillar that would probably love the texting vernacular of today.

"O R U (who are you)?" the caterpillar asks Alice.
"I hardly know," Alice responds. "I've changed so many times, you see."
"I do not C, explain yourself," says the caterpillar.
"I'm afraid I can't explain myself because I am not myself you know."
"I do not know," the caterpillar says.
"I can't put it any more clearly, for it isn't clear to me," Alice says.
"U, O R U (you, who are you)?" the caterpillar asks again.
"Everything is so confusing," Alice replies.[2]

Many people live out this scene. They're confused and don't know who they really are. "I'm trying to find myself," people say. Unfortunately when all is said and done, the question remains, "How will they know when they do?"

It is important to understand our identity because who we are shapes our entire lives.

---
[2] Ibid

Many people spend their lives in the pursuit of an identity. Their existence is constantly swirling around creating and defending an identity that may change from year to year, decade to decade.

For example some people might define themselves through body image and health. Over the years, however, tight toned bodies become soft and saggy.

Some define themselves by relationships. Yet single can soon turn to married, parent, grandparent, or sadly, divorced or widowed.

Some people define themselves through power, prestige, and possessions. Nevertheless, rich and famous can turn to poor and penniless with an economic downturn or job loss.

The problem is that while people are searching for an identity by looking to themselves or others, these definitions will fail because the world says we're an accident of nature. This is the wrong-headed thinking of evolutionists who say we're nothing more than evolved and elevated pond scum.

There is, however, a way for us to find the answer. Go to the Creator, the one who created us. We were made by God, and for God. Any definition other than the one given by God is going to disappoint, bringing with it despair and destruction.

How will we be called?

Should we be described by our problems, or by God's promise?

Elizabeth, John the Baptist's mother, was once defined by her childless condition.

"Her who was called barren." (Luke 1:36)

Although she was called barren everywhere she went, God saw her differently. God saw her as a mighty woman of faith and soon-to-be mother of one of His most important and mighty prophets.

God never calls us by our problems or conditions. He has new and better names for us. We need not believe in the world's definition of who we are. Instead we should believe in God's definition and live our lives based upon His word.

"For I know the thoughts that I think toward you, says the Lord, thoughts of peace and not of evil, to give you a future and a hope." (Jeremiah 29:11)

Rather than living life based on our shortcoming and inabilities, we should live life based upon what Jesus did at the cross, setting us free from sin and death. When we come into the saving knowledge of Jesus Christ we are a son or daughter of the Most High God, and a partaker of His wonderful promises of an abundant life now and an eternal life in heaven.

In Psalms 8:4 King David asked, "What is man that You are mindful of him, and the son of man that You visit him?"

Think about how important we are to God that He should pay attention to us! Yet He does. He says we're very important.

It's important we take time and see what God says about who we are and why He values us so highly.

We are no accident

In the CBN.com article "You Are Not an Accident," Rick Warren says, "Your birth was no mistake or mishap and your life is no fluke of nature. Your parents may not have planned you, but God did."

To Jeremiah, the Lord said, "Before I formed you in the womb I knew you; before you were born I sanctified you; I ordained you a prophet to the nations." (Jeremiah 1:5)

God set us apart and made us special. Before we were even born, before we were even conceived, before we were even a gleam in our parents' eyes, God knew and set each of us apart for His glory and good work. This is what "sanctified" means. It's the Hebrew word for something or someone that's holy, dedicated, consecrated, and separated for God's use and purpose.

God created us especially for Himself, and He is saying we have great worth, because He created us for Himself.

King David understood this worth and praised God for this truth.

"I will praise You, for I am fearfully and wonderfully made; marvelous are Your works." (Psalms 139:14)

God says we are special and no accident; but there's more. We have been on His mind for a long time, even before the creation of the world.

We are God's masterpiece

"For we are His workmanship, created in Christ Jesus for good works, which God prepared beforehand that we should walk in them." (Ephesians 2:10)

Workmanship in Greek is "poiema." It is where we get the word poem. It means something that has been made. God made us special, like a work of art, which is why some translations use the word, "masterpiece."

"Wait a second, this can't be right," we often insist. "I don't look or feel like a masterpiece. My life is not a da Vinci or Michelangelo. It's more like a Picasso."

We tend to only see our flaws or the things we wish we could change. But not so with God! We are God's work of art, His poem, His masterpiece, and He's not finished yet.

In Philippians 1:6 the Apostle Paul says, "Being confident of this very thing, that He who has begun a good work in you will complete it until the day of Jesus Christ."

God won't be finished with us until we're in His presence. Until then, we're a continuing work of His grace and mercy. We still sin, have trials, tribulations, and may be apathetic in our relationship with Christ, but that doesn't stop God. He's still working His grace and mercy in our lives.

God has begun a work to shape us to the image of Christ and He will not stop until He's finished. That won't happen until we're with Him in heaven.

Take a moment to look at God's work around you. Look at the shimmering beauty of a starlit sky. Look at the magnificence of a sunrise or sunset on the mountains as God paints the sky with the varying colors of blue, red, pink, purple, and orange.

In one of our men's Bible studies, someone commented on how beautiful the picture was on our church's Facebook page. It looks through an open door onto the majestic beauty of the ocean. Someone else disagreed.

"I can show you something better," he said. "Come with me out into the desert and watch the sunrise in all its beauty."

While beauty may be in the eye of the beholder, the truth is that all of it is beautiful, because it's all part of God's wondrous creation. But God's greatest masterpiece isn't the sunrise or sunsets. Nor is it the starry sky or the majestic mountains. God's greatest masterpiece is us.

God created us in His image and according to His likeness. We aren't some afterthought. We are His finishing touch. How beautiful is that?

Once we were a mess but now we're God's work of art, signed by His Spirit when we came to know Jesus Christ as our Savior and Lord. He has created each of us individually as His unique masterpiece to do His will on earth.

When we look in the mirror, we shouldn't sell ourselves short or see only our faults and failures. We should see ourselves as God's masterpieces that He's perfecting in His grace and mercy.

When we stand in front of the mirror we should make this Scripture personal and acknowledge, "I am God's masterpiece."

In fact, go even further and use your name saying, "_____ is God's masterpiece, created in Christ Jesus for good works, which God prepared beforehand that I should walk in them."

A new creation in Christ Jesus

"Therefore, if anyone is in Christ, he is a new creation; old things have passed away; behold, all things have become new." (2 Corinthians 5:17)

Once we were messes, but now we're God's masterpieces. Once we were sinners steeped in our sins, but we've been redeemed and are saints.

There's something exciting when we think about starting over because we've all messed up. All of us have said and done things we're embarrassed about, things we wish we could take back, things we wish we could do over.

Guess what. That's what being in Christ is all about. It's about forgiveness, grace, and mercy.

It's about finding hope when all hope seems lost. It's where we've messed up once again and think, "What's the use of trying?"

But in Christ we are new creations and God's desires to give us a future and a hope that is completely different than what we've known. It's a future hope, not only for right here and now, but also a hope of heaven where all the bad things, all the suffering, sorrow, and pain are gone. A place of no more tears or regrets. The old spirituals call it "The Land of No-Mores."

This is what we can look forward to even though we've messed up, because we are new creations in Christ Jesus. Paul didn't say a "perfect" creation, just new. We might say re-created by God to start living a brand new life.

When we come to Jesus Christ, asking Him to be our Savior and Lord, the Bible says we're not our own, but rather we've been bought with a price (1 Corinthians 6:19-20), and the price was the blood Jesus shed upon the cross.

There is a story about a man who wanted to buy an old, run down warehouse. The owner said he would clean the warehouse up and replace all the broken doors and windows.

"Don't worry about it," said the buyer. "I'm not buying it for the way it is now. I have completely new plans for it."

That's what God wants to do for us. He paid an exorbitant price for us on the Cross of Calvary as Jesus took our place and died the death we deserve.

But He didn't purchase us to keep us as we were, but to make us into something special and great. God wants to make us into new creations, what He originally intended when He created humanity before sin marred and broke what He created. God sees something more in each of us, something we may not see, and He is at work behind the scenes molding us into that new creation.

We are mighty men and women of valor

Every Sunday morning at our church services we repeat a biblical maxim that comes from Gideon's encounter with God, and a verse found in the Apostle John's first letter. This maxim reveals who we are in the Lord. Take a moment and say this out loud and repeat it every day.

"We are mighty men and women of valor because we are greater in the eyes of God than we are in our own eyes. While our hearts may condemn us, God is greater than our hearts and knows what truly lies within." (Judges 6:11-16; 1 John 3:20)

This adage came when our men's group attended the Foursquare Men's Camp in 2011. The speaker was talking about our worth, and he kept repeating, "We are greater in the eyes of God than we are in our own eyes."

I'm not much on slogans and philosophical feel-good statements unless they have a strong biblical foundation. The next morning while the guys were mulling around, trying to keep warm and waiting for a hot cup of coffee, I spent some time wondering about this statement.

I sat down and began reading First John. When I came to chapter three I read, "For if our heart condemns us, God is greater than our heart, and knows all things." (1 John 3:20)

Later that day we looked at the story of Gideon and there it was. God had wrapped this identity of who we are with a nice red ribbon. Gideon saw himself in a completely different light than God.

Gideon didn't think highly of himself or his capabilities. One day he was off by himself threshing grain in a wine press so he wouldn't alert the Midianites who would have come and taken it away. It was then the Lord came to Gideon and said, "The Lord is with you, you mighty man of valor!" (Judges 6:12)

I can just see Gideon looking over his shoulder to see if someone had suddenly come up from behind, because surely the Lord couldn't have been talking to him.

Gideon asks if the Lord was truly with them why were they in subjection to the Midianites?

The Lord said, "Go in this might of yours and you shall save Israel from the hand of the Midianites. Have I not sent you?"

"O my Lord, how can I save Israel?" Gideon asks. "Indeed my clan is the weakest in Manasseh and I am the least in my father's house."

Gideon was saying he was the lowest of the low. In fact, in Israel you couldn't get much lower. Think of it as a ladder with Gideon seeing himself below the bottom rung.

Unfortunately, too many of us see ourselves in the same light. The Bible tells us not to think more highly of ourselves than we should (Romans 12:3), but sometimes we take this to the extreme.

I remember someone saying, "I'm nothing but puffed up dust."

After a while I asked, "Yes, but who puffed you up?" adding later, "It was God who puffed you up with the Holy Spirit. So you are greater than you think."

This young man suffered from a mistaken identity. He saw himself as a sinning saint.

We are saints who sin

"To all who are in Rome, beloved of God, called to be saints." (Romans 1:7)

We are sinners saved by grace meaning we are saints who sometimes sin. This goes back to our being a new creation in Christ. We are no longer who we were. Life is no longer lived for ourselves but for God through Jesus Christ who lives inside us.

No longer are we sinners who have been graciously forgiven. We are saints – holy, righteous, set apart by God – who still also happen to sin.

If we continue to think of ourselves only as sinners, guilt will eat us alive. We'll live in constant fear of condemnation, not realizing that for believers in Christ on Judgment Day, it isn't punishment we'll receive, but rewards.

We are saints who still sin; therefore, sin will always be a part of our daily life.

"If we say that we have no sin, we deceive ourselves, and the truth is not in us," the Apostle John said. (1 John 1:8)

While sin is part of our life, we no longer need to be identified by it. Rather we're to be identified as saints who have been set aside by God for His great purpose and plan. We're saints who still have the sinful nature within until the day when we meet the Lord in heaven once this life is over.

Therefore we should live our lives always looking forward to our new identity and God's new name for us. Who we are in the Lord makes all the difference as to how we live now and for all eternity.

Knowing who we are on earth is important to our spiritual transformation. There is another identification, however, that makes the process complete.

Who we are in heaven

For all of us there is more than just viewing ourselves as God's original masterpiece, a new creation in Christ, a mighty man or woman of valor, and a saint who occasionally sins. There is more, much more.

There is eternity, and in eternity God has a new name for us. It is His name, and who we will be for all eternity.

"He who has an ear, let him hear what the Spirit says to the churches. To him who overcomes I will give some of the hidden manna to eat. And I will give him a white stone, and on the stone a new name written which no one knows except him who receives it." (Revelation 2:17)

"He who overcomes, I will make him a pillar in the temple of My God, and he shall go out no more. And I will write on him the name of My God and the name of the city of My God, the New Jerusalem, which comes down out of heaven from My God. And I will write on him My new name." (Revelation 3:12)

In biblical times names meant something. They spoke of a person's character. We also see God giving people new names to match their new role and/or responsibility.

It began with Abram and Sarai. God changed their names to Abraham and Sarah, which according to His own description said they would be the father and mother of many nations. (Genesis 17:5, 15-16)

Later, to Abraham's grandson, Jacob, whose name means deceiver, God changed his name to Israel, or one who prevailed with God, and upon whom the Jewish nation would descend. (Genesis 32:28)

The name God changed that holds the greatest significance is when Jesus changed Simon's name to Peter, which means, "rock" (Matthew 16:18). This is significant because Jesus gave to Peter one of God's own names. (Deuteronomy 32:3-4; 1 Samuel 2:2)

It's such a name we'll receive in heaven, a new name that not only represents our new nature, but also God's new name representing our new relationship with Him.

Throughout the Bible God records His many names revealing not only His nature and character, but also His relationship to humanity and to His people. But there is a name that's missing; a new name God will identify Himself with us in heaven.

And so in heaven we will receive two new names. The unique name God will give to us alone, (Revelation 2:17), and His new name. The name He will write upon each of us linking us to Him for eternity, (Revelation 3:12).

This could be one name with both aspects attached like many of the Old Testament names like Ezekiel, which has God's holy name, "El," attached to the word for strength. The name Ezekiel means "The Strength of God."

Or it could be two separate names. Right now my first name is Dennis and my last name is Lee, signifying my father's family. In heaven my first name will be God's new name for me, a name that will be for me and me alone. It's the name written on the white stone. My last name will be God's new name He will give to everyone signifying we're a part of His family.

Conclusion

Who are we? We are no accidents; we are God's original masterpieces, new creations in Christ Jesus, a mighty man or woman of valor, a saint who still occasionally sins. We must live our lives in accordance with our new identities, and live our lives in view of our new identity in heaven.

Who we are makes all the difference in the world as to our spiritual transformation.

REFLECTION AND DISCUSSION

1. When you look in the mirror, what do you see? Are there any hurtful descriptions others have placed upon you that you're still describing yourself by today?

2. Who does God say you are? (Ephesians 2:20; 2 Corinthians 5:17)

3. Do you often feel like you're an afterthought with God? Explain! What does God's Word say? (Philippians 1:6)

4. How do you relate to the statement, "I'm a saint that sin?" What does this mean to you?

5. What does it mean to you that you've been made in the image and likeness of God Himself?

6. What one thing will you take away from this chapter and apply to your life?

Chapter Three

Scrubbed And Cleansed

In the Chapter 2 we looked at our identity in Christ, who we are as Christians and saw that we're God's masterpieces, His work of art in progress. We saw we're a new creation in Christ Jesus but not a perfect creation. We saw that while we're mighty men and women of valor, we're prone to doubts. While we're saints, we're saints that sin.

All this leads naturally to the next step in this journey, and it's nothing less than an old fashioned soul-scrubbing and heart-cleansing.

A popular adage "cleanliness is next to godliness," means personal hygiene is something held in high esteem. True cleanliness, however, doesn't come from washing the dirt from one's body. It's washing the dirt from one's soul.

The Lord said, "No amount of soap or lye can make you clean. You are stained with guilt that cannot be washed away." (Jeremiah 2:22 New Living Translation or NLT)

To get our souls scrubbed and hearts cleansed, we must repent and ask God to forgive our sins. We must change our hearts and minds to follow God fully.

Our cleansing process begins with debunking the myth, "We have to learn to forgive ourselves."

Forgiveness isn't about forgiving self

Psychologists, whether secular or Christian, tell us we must forgive ourselves. As good intentioned as they are and as good as this sounds, forgiving oneself isn't possible because we can't forgive ourselves. It's not within us and we're not powerful enough. If we think we are, we're guilty of idolatry, making ourselves out to be God.

Now, you're probably saying: "Wait a minute. That's a bit harsh!"

Yet, it's not meant to be. The Bible never says we can forgive ourselves. Forgiveness only comes from God. Only God can forgive sins. The Pharisees knew this truth. When Jesus told the paraplegic man his sins were forgiven, they accused Jesus of blasphemy.

"Who can forgive sins but God alone?" (Mark 2:7b)

The Pharisees knew the Scriptures and knew what God spoke through the prophet Isaiah.

"I, even I, am He who blots out your transgressions for My own sake and I will not remember your sins." (Isaiah 43:25)

Jesus knew this truth and knew something the Pharisees didn't. He was God in no uncertain terms.

"The Son of man has power on earth to forgive sins." (Mark 2:10b)

Conversely, the Apostle Paul explains the reason we're to forgive others is because God forgave us.

"Be kind to one another, tenderhearted, forgiving one another, just as God in Christ forgave you." (Ephesians 4:32)

So, if we are unable to forgive our sins, why do so many people say it's absolutely necessary? It comes from guilt. We do terrible things that we regret, things we wish we could forget but are unable to. So the experts say we need to forgive ourselves so our guilt will no longer eat us alive.

This is a Band-Aid solution, however. It doesn't go to the heart of the matter or deal with the root of the offense, which is the sin nature.

Forgiveness only comes from God. If God has forgiven us, we don't need to forgive ourselves. Instead we must freely accept God's forgiveness. There's nothing we can do to cleanse ourselves from sin, because Jesus already paid the price forgiving us from all our sins through His death upon the cross.

To receive God's forgiveness we must confess our sins to Him because while our sins may have hurt others, in the end they're committed against God and have hurt Him. So receive God's forgiveness and walk in the freedom it brings.

King David understood this. David sinned in his adulterous affair with Bathsheba, and again when he had her husband, Uriah, killed. Later he learned his sin was against every man, woman, and child who died due to war under his regime. God said one of the consequences of David's sin was that war would never depart the land. But David knew his sin was ultimately against God.

"Against You, You only, have I sinned, and done this evil in Your sight." (Psalm 51:4)

The devil uses forgiving oneself as a tool against us. The problem with this process of forgiving ourselves is we become so focused in the quest we're no longer seeking God's forgiveness but our own. When we believe we've forgiven ourselves, then we prevent God from doing His cleansing work through true forgiveness.

So where do we start this work of soul scrubbing and heart cleansing? How do we begin to receive God's forgiveness?

Forgiveness begins with confession

Our soul scrubbing and heart cleansing begins when we confess our sins to God.

In 1 John 1:9 the Apostle John made this clear. "If we confess our sins, He is faithful and just to forgive us our sins and to cleanse us from all unrighteousness."

But what does it mean to confess?

Webster's Dictionary defines confession as telling or making known a wrong. But it actually goes much deeper. In Greek to confess means to speak the same thing. But the same things as what? It means to speak the same thing God speaks by calling what we do by its real name. It's calling sin what it is, sin.

It's not calling the sin of homosexuality an alternative lifestyle. It's not calling drunkenness going out and having a good time. It's not calling fornication and adultery messing around.

By not calling sin for what it truly is, we fail to get real about our sin, and we run the risk of missing out on God's kingdom.

In Galatians 5:19-21 the Apostle Paul says, "Now the works of the flesh are evident, which are adultery, fornication, uncleanness, lewdness, idolatry, sorcery, hatred, contentions, jealousies, outbursts of wrath, selfish ambitions, dissensions, heresies, envy, murders, drunkenness, revelries, and the like; of which I tell you beforehand, just as I also told you in time past, that those who practice such things will not inherit the kingdom of God."

These are not the one-and-done sorts of sins. It's the continual act of sinning. It's the lifestyle of sinning. It's sinning as a way of life.

Before the Apostle John told us our need to confess, he tells us why.

"If we say that we have no sin, we deceive ourselves, and the truth is not in us." (1 John 1:8)

In Romans 3:23 the Apostle Paul said, "All have sinned and fall short of the glory of God."

While the blood of Jesus Christ has redeemed us, we still have within us the nature to sin. It was passed down from generation to generation all the away from Adam and Eve who started it all. To confess is to admit to God we've sinned and fallen short of His holy and righteous standards for living.

If we want to continue down the road to spiritual transformation we must make a choice. We can continue to conceal the truth of our sins, or we can confess them. Solomon explains the results of each.

"He who conceals his sins does not prosper, but whoever confesses and renounces them finds mercy." (Proverbs 28:13 NIV)

There are consequences when we fail to confess our sins. The primary consequence is guilt. Guilt is devastating. It leads to anxiety and depression, which, in turn, leads to a myriad of physical and emotional problems.

King David understood these consequences and used himself as an example.

"When I refused to confess my sin, I was weak and miserable, and I groaned all day long. Day and night Your hand of discipline was heavy on me. My strength evaporated like water in the summer heat." (Psalm 32:3-4 NLT)

Because King David refused to confess his sin he was an emotional and physical mess. When he finally admitted his guilt and sought God, however, his guilt was removed.

"Blessed is he whose transgressions are forgiven, whose sins are covered ... I acknowledged my sin to You and did not cover up my iniquity. I said, 'I will confess my transgressions to the Lord,' and You forgave the guilt of my sin." (Psalm 32:1, 5 NIV)

Confession of sins brings healing, joy and peace.

"Fear the Lord and turn your back on evil. Then you will gain renewed health and vitality." (Proverbs 3:7b-8 NLT)

We can venerate King David's beautiful confession.

"Have mercy upon me, O God, according to Your loving kindness; according to the multitude of Your tender mercies, blot out my transgressions. Wash me thoroughly from my iniquity and cleanse me from my sin." (Psalm 51:1-2)

"Make me hear joy and gladness, that the bones You have broken may rejoice ... Restore to me the joy of Your salvation, and uphold me by Your generous Spirit." (Psalm 51:8, 12)

Confessing our sins to God removes the guilt and shame attached to them, bringing healing, joy, and peace. Confession is the first step in this process of soul scrubbing and heart cleansing. But we can't stop there. Confession needs to be immediately followed up by the second step, repentance.

God changes us through repentance

People generally find themselves trapped in a vicious cycle of sinning and confessing. Day after day they cry tears of sorrow only to find themselves doing the exact thing once again. Apostle Paul explained it best.

"When I want to do good, I don't. And when I try not to do wrong, I do it anyway." (Romans 7:19 NLT)

The cry of our hearts should be, "I want to change. I need to change. I have to change."

And we can do it! We can change! We can break the cycle that finds us in constant despair!

No matter how long we've been in this cycle, no matter how long we've been trapped in this pattern of defeat, we can change. The accusations against us can be silenced. The lies spoken about us can cease. The chains that bind us can be broken.

There are a whole lot of different programs and methods available in society and the church to facilitate change, but God has only one way, repentance. It is a common theme found throughout the Bible.

"Repent and turn from all your transgressions so that iniquity will not be your ruin." (Ezekiel 18:30)

In Matthew 3:2 John the Baptist said, "Repent, for the kingdom of heaven is at hand."

In Luke 15:7 Jesus said, "There will be more joy in heaven over one sinner who repents."

Jesus told His disciples to preach repentance.

"So they went out and preached that people should repent." (Mark 6:12)

It was also the message of the early church.

"Repent therefore and be converted, that your sins may be blotted out, so that times of refreshing may come from the presence of the Lord." (Acts 3:19)

It's safe to say that God's method of change is through the act of repentance. In fact, repentance requires change. We can't repent without changing.

Repentance isn't some half-hearted, "Sorry God."

Repentance is the Hebrew word that means to turn, turn from the way we are going and start walking in the way and will of God. In Greek it means to have a change of mind. It means more than merely mental consent, however. It involves the whole of our beings; our minds, will, and emotions.

Sin, however, has us talking a good game. We say things like, "It's not really that bad," or "Who will know and besides, God will forgive me." And then there is the pièce de résistance, "Everyone else does it," or "How can it be so wrong when it feels so right."

But repentance takes these lies and shines the light of God's truth upon them. Repentance is the process of rejecting these lies and turning away from them in order to do what is right, turning away from sin and turning toward God.

True repentance isn't easy, however.

"Now I rejoice, not that you were made sorry, but that your sorrow led to repentance. For you were made sorry in a godly manner, that you might suffer loss from us in nothing. For godly sorrow produces repentance leading to salvation, not to be regretted; but the sorrow of the world produces death." (2 Corinthians 7:9-10)

Merely to shed tears or express emotion is what Paul refers to as worldly sorrow, but it isn't genuine repentance. The word sorrow brings with it the idea of pain. It's an internal hurting. It's an anguish of the soul. This is godly sorrow that leads to repentance and eternal life.

Godly sorrow brings brokenness before God making a person ready to make a change. We see this in King David and the cry of his heart at his sin of adultery with Bathsheba and the murder of her husband. In Psalm 51 he lays it all out. He says that just being sorry and offering the sacrifices isn't enough.

"For You do not desire sacrifice, or else I would give it. You do not delight in burnt offering. The sacrifices of God are a broken spirit, a broken and a contrite heart. These, O God, You will not despise." (Psalm 51:16-17)

Yet, even though repentance isn't easy, it is possible and available to all who genuinely seek it.

"Seek the Lord while He may be found, call upon Him while He is near. Let the wicked forsake his way, and the unrighteous man his thoughts; let him return to the Lord, and He will have mercy on him; and to our God, for He will abundantly pardon." (Isaiah 55:6-7)

Conclusion

So, where are you today? Are you still caught up in the rat race of sin and confession without change? If that is you, you may be asking where to begin.

The best place is with prayer, fasting, and an extended stay in God's Word, because there needs to be a genuine desire on our parts to see our lives and sins the way God sees them.

Today if we hear God's voice telling us to repent we must not delay. We must not harden our hearts any longer. Instead, we must acknowledge our state before God. Come to our senses, confess, and turn toward God and away from our sins.

"Today, if you will hear His voice, do not harden your hearts as in the rebellion." (Hebrews 3:15 NKJV cf. Psalm 95:7)

This gospel song should be taken to heart.

"I Have Decided to Follow Jesus"

"I have decided to follow Jesus
"I have decided to follow Jesus

Scrubbed And Cleansed

"I have decided to follow Jesus
"No turning back, no turning back."

"Though I may wonder, I still will follow
"Though I may wonder, I still will follow
"Though I may wonder, I still will follow
"No turning back, no turning back."

"The world behind me, the cross before me
"The world behind me, the cross before me
"The world behind me, the cross before me
"No turning back, no turning back."

"Though none go with me, still I will follow
"Though none go with me, still I will follow
"Though none go with me, still I will follow
"No turning back, no turning back."

This means once we confess and repent, once we become followers of Jesus Christ, there's no turning back to the old sinful lifestyle again.

In Luke 9:52 Jesus says, "No one, having put his hand to the plow, and looking back, is fit for the kingdom of God."

Today let's begin our soul scrubbing and heart cleansing. Remember, there's no turning back.

REFLECTION AND DISCUSSION

1. Is there a personal sin you cannot forgive? What is it? Since you don't have the power to forgive yourself, what do you need to do?

2. Have you been rationalizing your sin by calling it a politically correct name? To confess means to call it like it is. What do you need to confess and ask forgiveness of?

3. Once you've confessed your sins, now what? What things do you need to do to begin the repentance process?

4. Up to this point has your repentance been more "Sorry God," or has it been "Lord forgive me and show me what and how I am to change?" What should repentance look like?

5. Have you begun this journey but now find yourself back in your old ways and habits? What steps do you need to take to get back on the narrow path and walk in the ways of the Lord?

6. What one thing will you take away from this chapter and apply to your life?

Chapter Four

Aligning With God and His Word

When I turned sixteen, my father gave me the family car, a 1963 Buick Riviera. The gift was bad in a good sense. It was what we called a sleeper. On the outside the Buick didn't look like much, but on the inside it screamed and usually won races against more powerful muscle cars like the Malibu and Mustang. Unfortunately, I didn't know much about cars, except how to steer and press the gas pedal. So when the car started drifting to the right, I learned to drive with the steering wheel turned half way to the left to compensate. I thought something was broken. But my dad told me the car was simply out of alignment, and the tires needed to be rotated and realigned.

This is just as true with us, with our lives, as it is with automobiles. After a while our lives can get out of alignment just like our cars. We often find we have to go to the doctor to get a medical checkup, or to psychiatrist to get our emotions back on track, or to the chiropractor to get our spines realigned.

But what about our spiritual lives? They can get just as far out of balance as our physical and emotional lives. Unfortunately, most people don't recognize the problem in their spiritual lives and, as a result, too many fail to get their spiritual wheels rebalanced and realigned.

To help with this spiritual realignment a person doesn't have to make an appointment with a spiritual hermit who lives in a mountain cave in some foreign land. Instead, it just takes going back to God and the Bible, His instruction manual for life.

God and His word won't disappoint. God's Word deals with those issues of life that take us away from having true alignment with Him and from moving straight ahead on the narrow road leading to everlasting life.

Solomon knew the path of realignment started with God.

"Trust in the Lord with all your heart and lean not on your own understanding. In all your ways acknowledge Him and He shall direct your paths." (Proverbs 3:5-6)

Acknowledge in the Hebrew language means to get to know someone in an intimate way. The way a husband or wife gets to know their spouse. So when we stop trying to do everything ourselves, getting to know God more intimately, then He'll realign our lives and get us back on track.

In this unbelievably stress-filled world, a world that distracts more than defines where many are drifting aimlessly along, we need to get our priorities in line to live full, productive, and effective lives. We do this by getting spiritually realigned with God, to His word, His will, and His way. If we don't, we'll find ourselves out of balance and drifting dangerously close to the edge.

This reminds me of a story about the owner of an estate whose house was situated on a large hill. To get to the house, travelers had to take a road that wound around the mountain. One day the man's chauffer died and he had to find a new driver. During interviews the estate owner asked each prospective chauffer how close he could drive to the road's edge without going over.

"I can drive two inches from the edge without going over," the first applicant said.

"I can drive with the wheel at the very edge without going over," the second applicant said.

The third applicant said, "I will drive as far from the edge as I possibly can."

To the third applicant the owner exclaimed, "You're hired!"

In the next two chapters we'll discuss getting our spiritual lives aligned with God, His word, His will, and His way.

Everything begins with God.

Getting aligned with God

God is the One who created, formed, and made us who we are. The Bible says we've all been fearfully and wonderfully made.

This was not lost on King David, who wrote:

"For you created my inmost being; you knit me together in my mother's womb. I praise you because I am fearfully and wonderfully made; your works are wonderful, I know that full well. My frame was not hidden from you when I was made in the secret place. When I was woven together in the depths of the earth, your eyes saw my unformed body. All the days ordained for me were written in your book before one of them came to be." (Psalm 139:13-16 NIV)

King David and the Apostle Paul understood that God made us all with a special plan and purpose in mind.

"All the days ordained for me were written in your book." (Psalm 139:16 NIV) You were created "for good works, which God prepared beforehand that we should walk in them." (Ephesians 2:10)

God tells us how to get spiritually aligned with Him and avoid veering off course.

"For thus says the High and Lofty One who inhabits eternity, whose name is Holy: 'I dwell in the high and holy place, with him who has a contrite and humble spirit, to revive the spirit of the humble, and to revive the heart of the contrite ones.'" (Isaiah 57:15)

Those spiritually aligned with God and those with whom God aligns Himself with, have a contrite and humble spirit. King David knew this when he blew it with Bathsheba.

He said God really doesn't require a physical sacrifice in order to get right with Him, instead the sacrifice God is looking for is a broken heart and crushed spirit over their sin, Psalm 51:17.

A humble and contrite heart and spirit are what the Lord desires. Holiness also aligns us with God.

The prophet Isaiah said that it is on this road that we must walk. "And a highway will be there; it will be called the Way of Holiness. The unclean will not journey on it; it will be for those who walk in that Way." (Isaiah 35:8 NIV)

God has set a "high way," a way that is visible and unmistakable. It's called the Way of Holiness.

A person's holiness doesn't begin with a set of religious rules and regulations; it begins with the Lord Himself. He is holy and calls us to be the same, that is, separate from sin.

"But as He who called you is holy, you must also be holy in all your conduct, because it is written, 'Be holy, for I am holy.'" (1 Peter 1:15-16 cf. Leviticus 11:44-45)

Holiness belongs to the same word group as sanctification. It means to be separated and set apart for God. It implies living a life of service for God, conforming to and becoming like the Lord we serve.

To be holy, however, does not mean you'll have no sin. Within each believer, which the Bible identifies as a saint, another nature exists, the sinful nature.

The Apostle Paul questioned, "O wretched man that I am, who will deliver me from this body of death?" (Romans 7:24)

The Apostle Paul added that evil is always present messing up the works and trying to draw us away from holiness.

"For the good that I will to do, I do not do; but the evil I will not to do, that I practice. Now if I do what I will not to do, it is no longer I who do it, but sin that dwells in me. I find then a law, that evil is present with me, the one who wills to do good." (Romans 7:19-21)

Those on the road of holiness are not at peace with the sin dwelling within. In fact they hate and long to be free from its grip.

The more we grow in holiness, the more our hatred for sin will grow.

"Your commandments give me understanding; no wonder I hate every false way of life." (Psalm 119:104)

The Apostle Paul agrees saying, "Let there be no sexual immorality, impurity, or greed among you. Such sins have no place among God's people." (Ephesians 5:3 NLT)

Let's stop deceiving ourselves that we can continue to sin without consequences. God is holy and just and will not overlook sin. God hates sin and we must start hating sin as well; we have to quit trifling with it and excusing our sins away.

To hate sin and desire to live a holy life, a life separated unto God, will align you with God.

Being aligned with God is our goal and we must also align ourselves with his word, will and way.

Aligning with God's Word

Most of us want to get on the road of life, press the accelerator and go. A major problem, however, is we haven't taken the time to look at the instruction manual to find out how this life works and how we can stay on the narrow road. We've gotten so busy we put off reading the instruction manual until times are less hectic. Right now we just want to take this new life in Christ for a spin.

When a manufacturer makes a machine it also provides an instruction manual on how to operate it. This may seems like a crude analogy but God's Word is like an automobile's instruction manual. Most cars have a designer/creator and a manufacturer that provides an instruction manual telling the owner how to operate it correctly.

The Bible is God's instruction manual for life. As the Designer and Creator, the One who built us, only God knows how we operate and how to keep and maintain this life He's has so graciously given.

The Bible tells us not only how we are designed, but also how to operate the machinery to live a full and productive life. When we follow its instructions, then life will begin to operate the way God intended. Life will come together where everything works and we become spiritually healthy, happy, and a little more stable.

Reading and studying God's Word is the most transformational practice we can do, because we daily encounter our Creator.

The Bible provides directions for every avenue on which we may find ourselves; every path we take, and every other aspect of our lives.

When we disregard its instructions, trouble soon follows. Life seems to go awry. Disregarding God's instructions causes an imbalance and we become more confused, frustrated, and unhappy.

Many people go through life without ever referring to God's instruction manual. That's unfortunate, because it's the only thing that can help them live rich and fulfilled lives.

God doesn't reveal His will through emotions, nor communicates it through the changing philosophies of man. God reveals His will through His word, the Bible. It must be read and we must become familiar with it in order to get into alignment with God.

The Apostle Paul said, "All Scripture is given by inspiration of God, and is profitable for doctrine, for reproof, for correction, for instruction in righteousness, that the man of God may be complete, thoroughly equipped for every good work." (2 Timothy 3:16-17)

"Given by inspiration of God," more literally means the Lord breathed out the Bible. The Apostle Peter says prophecy didn't come by the will of man, but through holy men separated by God for His work who spoke and wrote the words as they were moved by the Holy Spirit, 2 Peter 1:21.

The Apostle Paul says the Bible is "profitable." That is, it is useful, beneficial, and advantageous for our lives in teaching what is true, reproving what isn't, along with correcting and instructing us on how to get and stay right with God.

The writer of Hebrews provides an analogy that shows us how useful and powerful God's Word is when it comes to keeping you on the straight and narrow.

"For the word of God is living and powerful, and sharper than any two-edged sword, piercing even to the division of soul and spirit, and of joints and marrow, and is a discerner of the thoughts and intents of the heart." (Hebrews 4:12)

God's Word is living and powerful. Like a scalpel in the hands of a skillful surgeon, it's cuts through the philosophies and thoughts of man that are filled with contradictions and lies. It gets to the heart and the spirit of God's will and way.

Literally it's alive and will pierce our hearts, and touch our souls to change the course of our lives.

Don't wait until it is too late; don't wait until a crisis hits to read the Bible. Read it daily and be prepared for the trials and tribulations that will come.

To travel down the road to everlasting life, the Bible cannot be ignored. It's much too powerful not to be used. If taken seriously it will realign your life with God, His will, and His way.

Nothing is more transformative than listening, reading, and studying God's Word, His instruction manual for life.

Conclusion

Getting aligned with God is crucial in this journey from this life and into enteral life with the Lord, and this alignment begins with getting ourselves aligned with His word.

And while this begins with getting aligned with His word, it doesn't stop there. We must also get ourselves aligned to God's will and way. This is what we'll be looking at in our next chapter.

After that we'll look at some practical advice to help make it happen in chapter six.

Reflection and Discussion

1. In what areas have you gotten yourself out of alignment with God? In what areas have you been drifting to the right or left of God's Word?

2. What excuses have you used to justify being in this condition? Does it involve your finances, relationship, or job?

3. What does the Bible say about these areas where you find yourself unaligned with God?

4. What does the Bible say about your need of realignment? How important is it to get your life realigned in these areas?

5. What can you do, and what steps can you take to get your life realigned with God?

6. What one thing will you take away from this chapter and apply to your life?

Chapter Five

Aligning With God's Will and Way

When I began having serious steering problems with my 1963 Buick Rivera I was fortunate because all it took to repair it was a simple wheel alignment, tire rotation, and rebalancing. The fix could have been much more labor-intensive and costly.

There are three primary wheel adjustments associated with a front-end alignment including the caster, camber, and toe. Each must be adjusted to ensure the wheels are properly aligned. You can't fix just one element such as the camber without adjusting or tweaking the others. Getting the wheels realigned on a vehicle isn't as simple as many may think.

With normal use, often in some abnormal driving conditions, drivers can expect a certain amount of wear and tear as they rack up thousands of miles. As time passes various automobile parts will need replacing along with tire rotation and balancing. The whole process is complicated because mechanics realign a car's wheels when the vehicle is empty. In real everyday driving, however, the vehicle is often loaded with the driver, passengers, fuel, and whatever else might be stuffed inside, all of which will have an impact on the car and its alignment.

The same is true when it comes to getting aligned with the will and way of God. Like a car's realignment, there are several elements that need to be in balance with the others to get properly aligned spiritually.

Further, realignment doesn't happen in a vacuum but in real life. It happens with family, friends, neighbors, co-workers, and even strangers. It happens with those we like, as well as those we dislike. It happens in the best of times, it happens in the worst of times, which is why a daily realignment to God's will and way through His word are so important; so we don't find ourselves broken down on the side of the road.

We must align with the will and way of God if we're ever going to successfully reach the ultimate goal that God created and intended for us without limping over the finish line.

Aligning with God's will

The Lord is crying out today as He cried out in the day of the prophet Isaiah who promptly answered God.

"Whom shall I send and who will go for us? Here am I! Send me." (Isaiah 6:8)

The questions many people ask today are: "What is God's will for my life? What has God called for me to do?"

Fulfilling God's purpose according to His will is extremely important. God wants us to be everything He has created us to be, so we can reach our God-given potential and destiny.

Too often when we're unsure of God's will we fill the void by making it up as we go along.

For years a farmer desired to be a preacher. One day while planting his crop he looked to the sky and noticed the clouds seemed to form a "P" and a "C."

He immediately interpreted the clouds as a sign from God telling him to "Preach Christ." As fast as he could, he sold his farm, started a small church, and became its pastor. A major problem, however, was that he was horrible at it. After a particularly bad sermon, his neighbor whispered in his ear, "Are you sure God wasn't telling you to Plant Corn?"

God wants us to know His will. He wants us to discover and understand it. His goal is to lead and keep us in the center of His will.

"Be very careful, then, how you live; not as unwise but as wise, making the most of every opportunity, because the days are evil. Therefore do not be foolish, but understand what the Lord's will is." (Ephesians 5:15-17 NIV)

"If this is true," people ask, "why isn't God's will laid out more clearly?"

It is! The problem is when we get to the specifics of how we fit, that's when things get sketchy.

We'll tackle how a person can know how they fit in the next chapter. For now, let's look at what God has revealed about His will, which is like a collage where many parts make up the whole. Elements of the collage are those things God definitely calls us to do. Consider them His overarching will.

Loving God

Loving God is the heart of what it means to be a believer in Him. It's the statement of faith for all Jews and it's what Jesus identified as the greatest commandment.

"You shall love the Lord your God with all your heart, with all your soul, and with all your strength." (Deuteronomy 6:4-5; cf. Matthew 22:37)

Now if this is God's will, how do we accomplish it? It's easy to say we love God, but how do we show it? You can't throw your arms around God in a hug and give Him a peck on the cheek.

Jesus knew this, so He issued a second commandment as a way of showing our love for God.

"You shall love your neighbor as yourself." (Matthew 22:39)

The way we show God how much we love Him is to love those He's placed in our paths. The way we give God a great big hug, is to give a great big hug to those God places in our lives.

God's will begins and ends with our loving Him with the whole of who we are and then loving others in the same way He loves us. This is exactly how the Apostle John explained it saying we ought to lay down our lives for others just as Jesus laid down His life for us.

"By this we know love, because He laid down His life for us. And we also ought to lay down our lives for the brethren." (1 John 3:16)

In John 15:13 Jesus said, "Greater love has no one than this, than to lay down one's life for his friends."

Being missionary

Whenever I bring up being missionary people automatically think I'm talking about "becoming" a missionary. But to be missionary is the same as being evangelistic, the calling of every believer in Jesus Christ.

Jesus said, "Go therefore and make disciples of all the nations." (Matthew 28:19)

After His death, burial, and resurrection Jesus said to his disciples:

"Peace to you! As the Father has sent Me, I also send you." (John 20:21)

God the Father sent Jesus to bear witness of Him in everything Jesus said and did. In the same way, Jesus is sending us to bear witness of His saving grace in everything we say and do.

When we accept Jesus Christ as Savior and Lord we become children of God, and the nature of a child is to share their joy with others. It doesn't matter who may be around, all a child wants to do is to share the joy of whatever new toy or discovery they've made.

This is the heart of a child and the type of heart we need to possess. Why do so many find it so difficult? Mainly because we've become inward focused, that is, looking out for number one, for our own needs and desires.

If the fear of being ridiculed, ostracized, persecuted, or losing family and friends is preventing us from being a witness for Jesus Christ, look to what Jesus said and be comforted.

"If the world hates you, you know that it hated Me before it hated you ... Blessed are you when they revile and persecute you and say all kinds of evil against you falsely for My sake. Rejoice and be exceedingly glad, for great is your reward in heaven, for so they persecuted the prophets who were before you." (John 15:18; Matthew 5:11-12)

Worshiping God

A story of little boy's birthday party is a good illustration of the way many worship God.

The boy invited his best friends over to play football and basketball, eat hot dogs and hamburgers, and celebrate with a large birthday cake and ice cream. Everyone sang "Happy Birthday" at the top of their lungs.

After opening his birthday presents the boy took all his friends to the local high school basketball game to which he had paid everyone's admission. He envisioned his friends all sitting together eating popcorn and drinking soda while rooting for their favorite team. Once inside, however, his friends left him and scattered to sit with others.

We treat God much the same way in our time of worship. We go to church where God is the guest of honor. We give Him our routine gift, the tithe; we sing him a couple of songs, and listen to a message from His word. When we leave, however, we totally neglect Him, even though He paid the admission price for us to get into heaven. The saddest part is we don't see what we're doing.

We think and act as though we've fulfilled our religious obligation.

Worship is an Anglo-Saxon word better pronounced "worthship." It means to give worth or reverence to something or someone. In Greek and Hebrew it means to bow down in humility and submission.

To worship God is to humble ourselves in submission to Him. It's expressing the same attitude as that of John the Baptist.

"He must increase but I must decrease." (John 3:30)

Worshiping God is not an option; rather it's a command. When Satan told Jesus to worship him and all the kingdoms of the earth would be His, Jesus said:

"Away with you, Satan! For it is written, 'You shall worship the Lord your God, and Him only you shall serve.'" (Matthew 4:10)

True worship is not just going to a Sunday morning service. It is a way of life. What begins in the church needs to travel the streets and into our homes every day.

Growing spiritually

God designed all life to grow. From the moment of conception, God designed us to grow physically, emotionally, mentally, socially, and spiritually. Spiritual growth doesn't begin at conception, however, but when we're born again. Before this we were dead in trespasses and sin, as explained by the Apostle Paul.

"But God, who is rich in mercy, because of His great love with which He loved us, even when we were dead in trespasses, made us alive together with Christ, by grace you have been saved." (Ephesians 2:4-5)

God is the source for spiritual growth, but we all have a responsibility as well. This dual aspect of God's will is expressed by the Apostle Peter's second letter.

First God gives us everything we will ever need to grow physically as expressed in the word "life," and spiritually as seen in the word "godliness."

"His divine power has given to us all things that pertain to life and godliness, through the knowledge of Him who called us by glory and virtue." (2 Peter 1:3)

God has given us everything including the faith to believe. God tells us to add to this faith a set of virtues so we can live a bountiful and fruitful life.

"But also for this very reason, giving all diligence, add to your faith virtue; to virtue knowledge; to knowledge self-control; to self-control perseverance; to perseverance godliness; to godliness brotherly kindness, and to brotherly kindness love. For if these things are yours and abound, you will be neither barren nor unfruitful in the knowledge of our Lord Jesus Christ." (2 Peter 1:5-8)

Jesus makes it clear in John 15:5 that we can do nothing without Him but we need to commit ourselves to grow in our conduct and character.

Serving God

Through the parable of the sheep and goats Jesus taught about the coming judgment. The Lord uses our service to others to separate the good from the bad. In serving others we are actually serving God.

"When I was hungry and thirsty you gave me something to eat and drink. And when I was naked and sick you clothed and took care of me. When I was a stranger you invited me in. When I was in prison you came to visit," said the Lord.

"When did we do this for you Lord?" replied the people.

"Assuredly, I say to you, inasmuch as you did it to one of the least of these My brethren, you did it to Me." (Matthew 25:40)

It's in our service to others that we serve God. This is how God created us. It's a part of our spiritual DNA as the Apostle Paul explains.

"For we are His workmanship, created in Christ Jesus for good works, which God prepared beforehand that we should walk in them." (Ephesians 2:10)

God designed us with unique temperaments, personalities, characteristics, abilities, and capabilities. We are unique in order to fulfill God's purpose.

The Apostle Paul explains we must be plugged into God who works His will within us with the purpose to effect a godly change in this world.

"For it is God who works in you both to will and to do for His good pleasure." (Philippians 2:13)

So let the light of Jesus shine through your uniqueness so that God will be glorified.

"Let your light so shine before men, that they may see your good works and glorify your Father in heaven." (Matthew 5:16)

To get aligned with God's will we must get tuned into God, like tuning a car radio to the right station to receive its message. We must tune our lives to God and His word to know, understand, and align ourselves with His will.

You needn't be afraid of God's will because anything in the will of God is good.

"For I know the thoughts that I think toward you, says the Lord, thoughts of peace and not of evil, to give you a future and a hope." (Jeremiah 29:11)

"We know that all things work together for good to those who love God, to those who are the called according to His purpose." (Romans 8:28)

Be patient. God is still completing the work He has begun in you, as the Apostle Paul explains.

"Being confident that He who began a good work in you will carry it on to completion until the day of Christ Jesus." (Philippians 1:6 NIV)

Aligning with God's way

Instead of merely trying to make it through life, we should try living in a way that honors God, where we are aligned with His purpose. When we understand and start walking in the way of God our journey will start making more sense. Our lives will begin taking on a whole new meaning, be more substantive in nature.

Jesus in John 10:10 said He has come to give us life and that more abundantly.

King David told Solomon if he wanted to be successful, he'd have to find and walk in the ways of God.

"Keep the charge of the Lord your God, to walk in His ways, to keep His statutes, His commandments, His judgments, and His testimonies, as it is written in the Law of Moses, that you may prosper in all that you do and wherever you turn." (1 Kings 2:3)

But what is God's way so you can have this abundant life?

There are no easy answers especially when God says His ways are beyond our grasp.

"'For My thoughts are not your thoughts, nor are your ways My ways,' said the Lord. 'For as the heavens are higher than the earth, so are My ways higher than your ways, and My thoughts than your thoughts.'" (Isaiah 55:8-9)

Finding God's way is something for which we all need to strive. As explained in Psalm 103:7, God revealed his ways to Moses.

To know God's way we must deepen our knowledge of Him because if we don't understand the way of the Lord, then we'll never truly be able to serve Him as He wills.

If we want to know the way of God, then we must go to Jesus who is the way, the truth, and the life, John 16:33. It is through Jesus' teaching that He has shown the way to walk upon our journey of faith.

There are three ways Jesus tells us to walk.

The way of a child

It's sad to see how many Christians are becoming not only too big for their britches but also too big for Jesus.

When parents started to bring their children to Jesus, the disciples rebuked them. The disciples thought Jesus too important to spend time with children who would never fully appreciate Him and His teachings. Jesus, however, corrected them.

"Let the little children come to Me and do not forbid them; for such is the kingdom of God. Assuredly, I say to you, whoever does not receive the kingdom of God as a little child will by no means enter it." (Luke 18:16-17)

Children are utterly dependent and trusting of those in authority. To align to God's way is to become like a child, which is the way of simple trust and dependence.

When my granddaughter holds out her arms to me to be picked up, there's no doubt in her mind that I won't do it. She trusts not only that I will pick her up but also that I won't drop her. She is completely dependent on me to keep my word.

This is the same trust and dependency we need to have in our relationship with God. When we lift up our arms, when we venture forth in His will, He will be there to lift us up and never drop us. He will catch us when we fall and lift us up when we're down.

The Lord is standing right there with outstretched arms, waiting for us to reach out to Him. Do we have the faith of a child knowing that Lord will be there for us?

This is the way of a child and the way we align ourselves with God. We must put away any doubts that God won't be there, and put our faith in God who sees and cares for us.

God promised to always be there no matter what.

"I will never leave you nor forsake you." (Hebrews 13:4)

It's only when we're like a child that we'll be able to understand great spiritual truths. When those from the cities of Korazin and Bethsaida refused to repent and believe, Jesus admonished them.

"I praise you, Father, LORD of heaven and earth, because you have hidden these things from the wise and learned and revealed them to little children." (Matthew 11:25 NIV)

Unlike most adults, children do not require all the complicated and lengthy explanations before they're willing to believe. They're willing to accept the simple truth of God.

This doesn't mean we should be naïve and trust whoever and whatever we're told. That's not having childlike faith. That's foolish. Instead, we should trust God at His word through His word.

This is what the Bereans did. The Bible says they investigated what was being taught by the truth of God's Word.

"Now the Bereans were of more noble character than the Thessalonians, for they received the message with great eagerness and examined the Scriptures every day to see if what Paul said was true." (Acts 17:11 NIV)

They didn't go to their theology books but to the Bible. They had the simple trust that God's Word is true. They trusted in and were dependent upon their heavenly Father at His word.

We all must approach our relationship with the Lord as children, trusting that He will supply what we need when we need it as the Apostle Paul explained.

"And my God shall supply all your needs according to His riches in glory by Christ Jesus." (Philippians 4:19)

To align ourselves with God we need to recover those childlike qualities of total dependency and trust in Him.

The way of a servant

The Apostle Paul said we should possess the same attitude that was on full display in Jesus' life, the attitude of a humble servant.

"Let this mind be in you that was also in Christ Jesus, who, being in the form of God, did not consider it robbery to be equal with God, but made Himself of no reputation, taking the form of a bondservant, and coming in the likeness of men." (Philippians 2:5-7)

The way of a servant is the way of humble servitude. A way Jesus Himself demonstrated when He picked up a towel and basin of water and washed the disciples' feet.

Jesus took upon Himself the lowest position within the hierarchy of household slaves.

"I have set you an example that you should do as I have done for you." (John 13:15)

Jesus, the second person of the Godhead, bent down and served as an example in how we are to walk in the way of a servant, and then He said we'd be blessed when we do, John 13:17.

The way we align ourselves to God's way is to take the way of a servant.

James and John came to Jesus asking to sit at His right and left hands when He came into His kingdom. Jesus acknowledged their request.

"Whoever wants to become great among you must be your servant and whoever wants to be first must be slave of all. For even the Son of Man did not come to be served, but to serve, and to give his life as a ransom for many." (Mark 10:43-45 NIV)

Our goal should be to humbly serve others with Jesus' attitude even when it may be overlooked or taken for granted.

"For God is not unjust to forget your work and labor of love which you have shown toward His name, in that you have ministered to the saints, and do minister." (Hebrews 6:10)

The great conductor, Leonard Bernstein, was asked, "What's the hardest instrument to play?"

"The second fiddle," Bernstein replied without hesitation. "I can get plenty of first violinists, but to find someone who can play the second fiddle with enthusiasm — that's a problem. And if we have no second fiddle, we have no harmony."

Everyone wants to be number one. No one likes to humble themselves in the service of others. We'd much rather be served. But true greatness isn't found in being served but in serving others, as Jesus said.

"If anyone serves Me, let him follow Me; and where I am, there My servant will be also. If anyone serves Me, him My Father will honor." (John 12:26)

When we realize God's way is the way of humbly serving others, and we follow that way, we'll not only be aligned with God, but we'll also have an impact on the world around us.

The way of the cross

The problem with the narrow way is most people don't like its defining quality; it's narrowness. They want options. They want off-ramps where they can get off and indulge themselves. But Jesus made it clear that keeping to the straight and narrow is the only way, and He did so by saying that His way is the way of the cross.

"If anyone desires to come after Me, let him deny himself, and take up his cross daily and follow Me." (Luke 9:23)

To deny ourselves means to lose what we want in order to become everything Jesus wants us to be. This, however, goes against the grain. We want to make the decisions for our lives, rather than giving up that right to Jesus.

The way of the cross is the way of total commitment.

Unfortunately many want to follow Jesus for what they can get. They really like Jesus, but they don't want to serve the poor, to forgive and pray for those who hurt them, to love their enemies, or bear another person's burdens.

They will follow Jesus as long as they're not asked to go to church, to give of their resources, or to stop having sex outside the biblical definition of marriage.

In other words, "I'll follow, but don't ask me to change."

They only want a part-time gig or halfway commitment. But Jesus says it's all or nothing.

Jesus wanted to make sure those who would be His followers must be willing to live lives of sacrifice, to be living sacrifices in the service of God's kingdom.

Jesus wasn't trying to garner popular support. There were plenty of people who hung around Him for what they could get. Jesus, however, wanted men and women who would be trustworthy in times of crisis and unwavering in their devotion to God.

"Take up your cross and follow Me," Jesus said.

This isn't some inconvenience or a problem someone may be facing. Nor is it looking and acting like a Christian, whatever that may be. It's doing what Jesus tells us to do.

The way of the cross is following Jesus, doing what He says, not once in a while when it suits us, but all the time. It's a way of life we choose.

"For whoever desires to save his life will lose it, but whoever loses his life for My sake will save it. For what profit is it to a man if he gains the whole world, and is himself destroyed or lost." (Luke 9:24-25)

Jesus is saying this life is a choice so we need to choose wisely.

We can save what we have. We can cling to every last breath, dollar, possession, and relationship. The only problem is that when we find everything we want, we'll also find emptiness. Everything we gain will slip through our grasp, and all that we'll end up with are hollow and empty lives; lives that will mock our very existence when death comes knocking.

Or we can lose our lives. We can give ourselves away, give up the right to ourselves, and make a total commitment to Jesus. In the end our lives won't be wasted but saved. We'll find contentment and satisfaction, and when death comes knocking we'll realize there is more than this life we live, and that heaven is our real home.

While the way of the cross isn't easy, it's rewarding and the only way to live.

Missionary Jim Elliot, who was martyred for his faith attempting to evangelize the Huaorani people of Ecuador said, "He is no fool who gives up what he cannot keep to gain what he cannot lose."

Conclusion
In the past two chapters we've looked at our need to be aligned to God, His word, His will, and His way. It's the practical "how to" that's now needed. This is what the next chapter delves into as we look at some practical advice in this process of alignment.

REFLECTION AND DISCUSSION

1. Have you ever found yourself broken and on the side of the road of life? Where and when? What were the contributing causes?

2. What is God's overall will for your life? How has God made you to fulfill this will? What gifts and talents did God give you to carry out His will?

3. What steps can you take to love others in the way outlined in the Bible so you can show God how much you love Him?

4. What has stopped you from being missionary to your family, friends, co-workers, neighbors, and strangers?

5. What can you do to better understand the will and way of God for your life? What does it mean to be more child-like and more like a servant, taking the way of the cross?

6. What one thing will you take away from this chapter and apply to your life?

Chapter Six

The Process of Alignment

In order to get the most out of our cars, to improve fuel efficiency and increase road safety, we should pay attention to how our vehicles respond to the road. No matter how careful we are in maintaining our vehicles, however, over time with the normal wear and tear from driving, not to mention the unavoidable accidents that may occur along the way, problems are bound to arise. Aligning wheels and balancing tires are important steps in keeping a vehicle in good condition.

Just as we should keep our automobile wheels in alignment, it's important to understand the need to be in alignment with God and His word. Unfortunately, many believe that aligning themselves with God's will and way is too difficult. They'd much rather sit in the pews on Sunday morning, put in their required church time, and live life their own way and on their own terms.

They prefer the comfort and security of the familiar. God, however, wants His people to be in the right place at the right time to fit with His plan and attain His kingdom. This is why getting in proper alignment with the will and way of God is so important.

Just as God told Abram to leave his father's country and go to a land He would later reveal, God can also give us clear directions for life. God doesn't leave a trail of breadcrumbs hoping we get from point A to point B. He gives us specific instructions to align with His will and way so His blessing can pour unfettered into our lives.

In this chapter I'll provide practical advice on how we can align ourselves to the will and way of God. Most of this we already know but it won't hurt to have a reminder. This was Apostle Peter's assessment as well.

"For this reason I will not be negligent to remind you always of these things, though you know and are established in the present truth." (2 Peter 1:12)

Being in God's Word

To align with God, His will and way, we must get aligned with His word. To continue on the journey toward spiritual transformation, there will be times of darkness, uncertainty, and doubt through which only God's Word can light the way.

"Your word is a lamp to my feet and a light to my path." (Psalm 119:105)

Only God's Word can cut through deceptive emotions and Satan's destructive strategies and help us get to the heart of the matter.

"For the word of God is living and powerful, and sharper than any two-edged sword, piercing even to the division of soul and spirit, and of joints and marrow, and is a discerner of the thoughts and intents of the heart." (Hebrews 4:12)

God is the one who inspired everything in the Bible. That's why it's called God's Word. It contains everything we need to live a meaningful life.

"All scripture is given by inspiration of God and is profitable for doctrine, for reproof, for correction, for instruction in righteousness that the man of God may be complete, thoroughly equipped for every good work." (2 Timothy 3:16-17)

God's Word was literally breathed out and into the men who wrote the Bible. As you read God's Word, the Holy Spirit reveals His

The Process of Alignment

purpose and direction for our lives. It's analogous to a sighted guide for a blind snow skier. A skier, who can see, skis behind or next to the blind skier shouting about what is ahead and how to proceed without mishap.

By following the shouted instructions, the blind skier can successfully navigate the hill with all its bumps and curves. If he or she should fail to trust their sighted guide, however, or refuse to listen, thinking they know what's best, they are in for a disaster.

God's Word is our guide. As we read the Bible, God, through the Holy Spirit, instructs us what direction to take to successfully navigate our journey of spiritual transformation. If we fail to trust God's directions, we'll likely find ourselves in the woods plastered to a tree.

To know more of God's will and way for life, we then need to align ourselves with God's Word and fill our heart and minds with it.

Prayer and fasting

Having the right tools and knowledge of their use is critical to success in any endeavor. This is especially true in prayer when it's coupled with fasting. The combination increases our effectiveness as well as our spiritual powers by allowing us to know God's will and calling.

Fasting and prayer are central in successfully navigating through the many struggles of life, including getting free from bondage, Isaiah 58:6, and receiving deliverance in times of crisis, 2 Chronicles 20. It is also used to gain spiritual insight and receive God's wisdom and direction.

This can be seen in God's call to the apostles Paul and Barnabas to be missionaries to the gentiles. The Christians at Antioch fasted and prayed before sending them out.

"As they (the church leaders of Antioch) ministered to the Lord and fasted, the Holy Spirit said, 'Now separate to Me Barnabas and Saul for the work to which I have called them.' Then, having fasted and prayed and laid hands on them, they sent them away." (Acts 13:2-3)

Ezra was a Hebrew scribe God chose to return to Jerusalem to rebuild His temple. King Cyrus gave him great favor, but Ezra knew God's strength and wisdom were necessary to get the temple rebuilt. So he proclaimed a fast to seek and ask the right way to go.

"Then I proclaimed a fast there at the river of Ahava, that we might humble ourselves before our God, to seek from Him the right way for us and our little ones and all our possessions ... So we fasted and entreated our God for this, and He answered our prayer." (Ezra 8:21, 23)

To fast is to abstain from food and/or drink. When we fast, usually for a specific period of time, we seek the Lord by denying the physical and focusing on the spiritual.

Adding fasting to prayer cleans out the spiritual blockages and allows us to spiritually get connected to God where we can hear the still small voice of the Lord.

This was the testimony of the prophet Elijah. For 40 days he went without food until he arrived at Mount Horeb. He went into a cave where he was able to hear God's still small voice over the commotion going on around him. (1 Kings 19)

Prayer and fasting are powerful tools but they're not part of some magical formula to gain God's favor. God cannot be forced or coerced. We will still have trials and tribulations in this world, John 16:33, but when we fast and pray God will strengthen us and give us the grace, mercy, and faith for the journey ahead.

Praising God

We are to enter into the Lord's presence with joyful songs of praise, Psalm 100.

The Process of Alignment

Praising God as we align ourselves to Him, His will, and His way adds power to the act.

P.U.S.H, which means, "Pray until something happens," explains the need to pray through problems. Let me recommend another P.U.S.H., "Praise until something happens."

This was how David handled the many difficulties and problems he faced. David's problems were definitely not average or run-of-the-mill. He faced outright hostility by those who wanted to kill him. His problems were those that nightly left his pillow soaked with tears.

David praised God when he prayed. He sang about his problems, and about his faith and trust in God to see him through his stressful times. They are called Psalms because they are literally songs and hymns.

In Psalm 22:3 we're told that God inhabits the praises of His people. Praise is a vehicle bringing us into the presence and power of the Lord God. It's one of the most effective ways through which we can find guidance.

Therefore, praise is much more than a song service on Sunday morning. It's a way of life for every believer in Jesus Christ. More, it's God's revealed will.

"Rejoice always, pray without ceasing, in everything give thanks; for this is the will of God in Christ Jesus for you." (1 Thessalonians 5:16-18)

When you praise God in everything and give Him thanks not only for the good but the bad as well, then you'll see God changing you into becoming more like Him.

Believers are called a holy and royal priesthood for the express purpose of offering praise to God, 2 Peter 2:9.

Therefore, let's offer to God a sacrifice of praise to replace the spirit of heaviness. Isaiah 61:3.

Getting alone with God

Getting alone with God is a way to allow God to talk with us without worldly distractions.

It isn't about escaping reality, nor is it to get away from responsibilities. It's about taking time to find how to live in our present reality by coming into the reality of God and allowing Him to renew our purpose.

Prison systems use the technique of solitary confinement. Getting alone with God is much the same, but not as a form of punishment. Instead it's meant to break the human will so that it can be aligned with God's will.

It is meant to weaken your bondage to the world and strengthen our dependence upon God. It helps set us free from the ways of the world that may be preventing us from more fully hearing and following God's will and way.

Getting alone with God was Jesus' way of aligning Himself with His Father.

When Jesus was in the Garden of Gethsemane, He left Peter, James and John to pray. Only then was He able to make this declaration, "O My Father, if this cup cannot pass away from Me unless I drink it, Your will be done." (Matthew 26:42)

Jesus knew the value of getting alone with God. Quite often He would go off by Himself to pray and get His Father's take on what He was to do.

Knowing the value of such alone time, Jesus showed and taught His disciples the same.

"Come aside by yourselves to a deserted place and rest a while." (Mark 6:30-32)

The Process of Alignment

In the Sermon on the Mount, Jesus, quoted in Matthew 6:6, said, "But you, when you pray, go into your room, and when you have shut your door, pray to your Father who is in the secret place; and your Father who sees in secret will reward you openly."

To be like Jesus, to follow His ways, you must learn to discipline yourself to get away from the worldly pressures and be alone with God. Let Him do His transformational work from within.

"And do not be conformed to this world but be transformed by the renewing of your mind that you may prove what is the good and acceptable and perfect will of God." (Romans 12:2)

Getting alone with God doesn't just happen. You have to be purposeful about it. You have to set time aside because the enemy will do everything he can to keep you busy and occupied with what is not of God.

These don't have to be long periods of time, because then you'll never do it. Instead plan small segments during the day to get away with God and pray.

"Speak, Lord, for Your servant hears." (1 Samuel 3:10)

Seeking Godly counsel

We are not commanded to live this Christian life alone. No one does well by themselves. Even the Lone Ranger had Tonto.

Part of our human nature wants only to seek out those who agree with us and confirm our desires. This, however, isn't the way or the will of God. We need others who will honestly speak to our situations. Therefore we don't need just any counsel; instead we need to seek out godly counsel from those who can give us godly advice from God's Word.

In 2 Timothy 4:3 Apostle Paul said people will not always endure sound teaching and counsel, but, because of itching ears, they'll go to those who will tell them what they want to hear.

We must purpose to seek those who believe in Jesus Christ and who have been gifted by God to give godly counsel. We should likewise be quick to reject any advice that's not supported by God or goes against his word.

Godly counsel should give you God's perspective. God word says:

- "A wise man will hear and increase learning, and a man of understanding will attain wise counsel." (Proverbs 1:5)

- "Where there is no counsel, the people fall; but in the multitude of counselors there is safety." (Proverbs 11:14)

- "The way of a fool is right in his own eyes, but he who heeds counsel is wise." (Proverbs 12:15)

- "Get all the advice and instruction you can, and be wise the rest of your life." (Proverbs 19:20 NLT)

Seek out godly counsel, it will help you become wise and find God's leading, purpose, will, and way for your life.

Getting involved

I come from the school of thought that says if you believe in something, then put your time, energy, and effort into it. This was never as true as when I came to believe in Jesus Christ.

I put everything I had into what the Lord said, especially when it came to serving others. When Jesus told the parable of the sheep and goats and how, when we serve others we serve the Lord, I jumped right in and started serving God in my church.

The Process of Alignment

I wasn't sure exactly what my calling was, but when a need arose, I was ready and willing to meet it. I started out being an usher and then taught in the children's ministry. Because of my business background I helped set up the church's books and helped start the church's bookstore. I began teaching a home fellowship and also in the church's bible school. While I made mistakes, I grew from them and the Lord continued to define my calling, to be a teacher of His word.

Far too many, however, are "waiting" on the Lord, but they are doing it the wrong way.

"Those who wait on the Lord shall renew their strength; they shall mount up with wings like eagles, they shall run and not be weary, they shall walk and not faint." (Isaiah 40:31)

The focus is on our need to wait upon the Lord. But what exactly does that mean? The word wait is not a passive noun. It's an active verb, which means waiting is an action.

Think of it this way. Those who serve us at our favorite restaurant are called "waiters." Their function is to serve us, not wait for us to serve them.

That's what it means to wait upon the Lord. It's to serve in whatever capacity is needed within the local church, allowing God to direct and show us His will through our involvement.

Others have gotten tired and become content with sitting in the pews letting others do the work.

"I've already put my time in," they say, "Let someone else do it."

But that's not what God called upon his protégé Timothy to do, who most likely was feeling the same way.

"These things command and teach. Let no one despise your youth, but be an example to the believers in word, in conduct, in love, in spirit, in faith, in purity. Till I come, give attention to reading, to exhortation, to doctrine. Do not neglect the gift that is in you, which was given to you by prophecy with the laying on of the hands of the eldership." (1 Timothy 4:11-14)

"For this reason I remind you to fan into flame the gift of God, which is in you through the laying on of my hands." (2 Timothy 1:6 NIV)

Basically Paul was saying, "Don't let others dictate your calling, and don't neglect God's gift and calling upon your life, instead fan the glowing embers back into a roaring flame."

The only way this is accomplished is by being a servant of the Lord, serving Him through serving others.

Take that first step and get involved. Let the Lord define and refine His calling upon your life. Don't wait for others to ask you; when you see a need fill it.

Counting the cost

To fulfill God's will to pick up your cross and follow Him will cost.

"For which of you, intending to build a tower, does not sit down first and count the cost, whether he has enough to finish it." (Luke 14:28 NKJV)

A chicken and a pig were walking down a country road when they saw a sign advertising a benefit breakfast to feed the poor.

"We should give them a ham and egg breakfast," the chicken said.

"For you it only requires a contribution," said the pig to put the brakes on the suggestion. "For me it's a total commitment."

The Process of Alignment

Some use Jesus' illustration to get out of fulfilling a need within the church or say the cost is too high. This, however, is not what Jesus meant.

A tower wasn't a luxury the people could do without. A tower was a necessity. It was used to look out over the fields to detect movement of a predator or an enemy coming against them. So they had to sit down and count the cost making sure they had enough to build the tower and not abandon it half way through the project. There's nothing more tragic than a ministry that closes down.

"No one, having put his hand to the plow, and looking back, is fit for the kingdom of God." (Luke 9:62)

Having good intentions isn't enough; neither is starting well. We have to finish what we've started when we came into the faith of Jesus Christ. It's all about finishing; it's all about making a commitment and finishing what we start. It's all about paying the price, picking up our cross and following Jesus.

Fulfilling God's will and calling on our life doesn't come easy. In fact, it comes with a price tag. It's going to cost us something. It may cost us time and energy. It may cost us finances or even our job. It may cost us a relationship or two.

There's more to being a Christian than just saying you believe. Jesus had lots of people following Him, but most weren't willing to count the costs and take up their crosses and follow. They were there for what they could get, not what they could give.

Whatever the costs, it's worth it in the end when you hear Jesus say, "Well done, good and faithful servant; you have been faithful over a few things, I will make you ruler over many things. Enter into the joy of your lord." (Matthew 25:23)

To count the cost is not a method to hide from God's call; rather it's to make sure you've got everything lined up to finish well.

When it comes to counting the costs, you may want to ask not what it will cost to follow Jesus, but rather what will it cost not to follow Him.

Conclusion

Operating within the will and way of God through His word isn't a luxury; rather it's a necessity if we want to finish well our journey into eternity. To finish well means we have to run according to the rules, which occurs when we put into practice what the Bible says.

Therefore we need to take time daily to get into God's Word and let God's Word get into us. We need to get serious about prayer and fasting, and praising God for the good times as well as the bad times. We need to take time alone with God to hear His voice, to get godly counsel from others, and to get involved by serving God by serving others.

Let's begin today to get ourselves realigned to God, because no one is guaranteed tomorrow.

REFLECTION AND DISCUSSION

1. Have you ever taken time to fast and pray? What was the occasion and result? Is there something you need to fast and pray about today? What is it?

2. What specifically do you need to praise God for?

3. Have you scheduled time alone with God? Where will you go? How much time will you give to be alone with God in silence and solitude?

4. Is there someone you've made yourself accountable to? Why have you chosen them? Are they spiritually attuned to hear God for your life?

5. How are you waiting upon the Lord? How are you serving God in this time of waiting? Have you considered the costs, and exactly what are the costs?

6. What one thing will you take away from this chapter and apply to your life?

Chapter Seven

Filled and Overflowing

My wife complains how I always wait to the last second to fill my gas tank. She says it seems like I'm trying to see how far I can go before I run out of gas. But this is not a good strategy when it comes to our spiritual journey. We constantly need to keep our spiritual gas tank filled because we need all the energy possible to continue on this journey of faith God has called us upon.

So far in our journey to spiritual transformation, the journey from this earth to our eventual home in heaven where we'll hear the Lord say, "Well done good and faithful servant" (Matthew 25:2), we've seen our need to chose the narrow gate and narrow way leading to heaven. It is the road less traveled because it isn't an easy road to follow. The ending, however, is worth the difficulty.

We have also seen who we are in Christ and learned we are His masterpiece, new creations, mighty men and women of valor, and saints who, because of the sin nature residing within, need an old-fashioned soul-scrubbing and heart-cleansing through confession of sins and turning away from them in repentance.

In the last three chapters we looked at our need to get aligned with God, His word, His will, and His way, and the steps we can take to find His specific calling upon our lives.

And here's the kicker. The power to do this doesn't lie within us; rather it lies in God through the power of the Holy Spirit. Consider these biblical passages.

"You are of God, little children, and have overcome them, because He who is in you is greater than he who is in the world." (1 John 4:4)

This means the Holy Spirit residing within us is greater and mightier than Satan and his demonic hoard, along with anything and everything that can be thrown against us.

Here's what the Apostle Paul tells the church in Ephesus.

"That He would grant you, according to the riches of His glory, to be strengthened with might through His Spirit in the inner man." (Ephesians 3:16)

Paul is saying that within every believer there is tremendous power.

"Now to Him who is able to do exceedingly abundantly above all that we ask or think, according to the power that works in us." (Ephesians 3:20)

The power of the Holy Spirit enables believers to walk upon the narrow road, confess and turn away from their sins to live in spiritual victory. The power of the Holy Spirit is the power to stop living for the world and all its enticements, and start living for God.

"I say then, walk in the Spirit and you shall not fulfill the lust of the flesh. For the flesh lusts against the Spirit, and the Spirit against the flesh, and these are contrary to one another, so that you do not do the things that you wish." (Galatians 5:16-17)

The Christian life is not a once-in-a-while life. It is a way of life lived every minute of every day. This is what the Apostle Paul meant when he said, "Walk in the Spirit." It means continuously living life dependent upon the guidance and power of the Holy Spirit, and when we do our sinful nature will stop dominating our lives.

Being filled and overflowing with Holy Spirit power allows us to live effective lives for God.

Power to share your faith

Being filled and overflowing with Holy Spirit power allows us to effectively share our faith, helping others find and appreciate this life-changing faith.

In Acts 1:8 Jesus said, "But you shall receive power when the Holy Spirit has come upon you; and you shall be witnesses to Me in Jerusalem, and in all Judea and Samaria, and to the end of the earth."

The Holy Spirit empowers us to share our faith, boldly proclaiming the truth of Jesus Christ to this lost and dying world. This is witnessed throughout the book of Acts especially in the formation of the church.

We see this power at work in the Apostle Peter's life. Fifty days prior to this event Peter was terrified denying Jesus to a servant girl. Imagine a big burley fisherman cowering before a little girl. But fifty days later he's standing in front of thousands sharing the wonderful news of Jesus Christ. (Acts 2)

This was a direct result of the filling and overflowing presence of the Holy Spirit. On that day the Holy Spirit moved through the room where the disciples and followers of Jesus were staying and praying, lighting a fire over and, figuratively speaking, under each one of them. Afterward they immediately hit the streets proclaiming the wonderful works of God in the different languages of those listening.

Later, after healing a lame man at the gate called Beautiful that led into the temple, Peter and John were arrested, thrown into jail, and threatened. They were told never to speak in Jesus' name again. But Peter, John, and the church prayed.

"The place where they were assembled together was shaken; and they were all filled with the Holy Spirit, and they spoke the word of God with boldness." (Acts 4:31)

God gives us Holy Spirit power to effectively fulfill the "Great Commission" to go make disciples of all nations, baptizing them in the name of the Father, the Son, and the Holy Spirit, teaching them everything that Jesus commanded, Matthew 28:19-20.

There's a common denominator concerning these stories of receiving power to be an effective witness for Jesus. This power was given in direct response to prayer.

Power to enter God's presence

Being filled and overflowing with Holy Spirit empowers our prayer life allowing us to enter into the presence of God in ways we never imagined.

In Romans 8:26 the Apostle Paul says, "Likewise the Spirit also helps in our weaknesses. For we do not know what we should pray for as we ought, but the Spirit Himself makes intercession for us with groanings which cannot be uttered."

Paul adds in Romans 8:27, "Now He who searches the hearts knows what the mind of the Spirit is, because He makes intercession for the saints according to the will of God."

The Holy Spirit not only gives us the power to witness but also makes our prayers effective. The Holy Spirit helps our weakness when it comes to prayer because we naturally don't know how to pray, or what we should be praying for. Being the third person of the Godhead, the Holy Spirit knows the mind and will of the Father and Jesus toward us. Therefore He can effectively intercede on our behalf empowering us to seek the Father and Jesus to an even greater extent than we could on our own.

The Holy Spirit fills and overflows us with the faith to believe, something we desperately need because many of us don't feel as if our prayers are making it up to heaven or being at all effective. We read the Bible about the prayer life of great men and women of faith and when we compare our prayer experience it doesn't seem to measure up. So we feel disillusioned, disheartened, and just want to give up.

This is where the Holy Spirit helps. The Holy Spirit gives us the power to continue praying and believing God and His promises more than the circumstances surrounding us. The Holy Spirit knows what we're going through, and He groans right along with us. His groans, however, are not out of despair, but in a language all His own. It's a language heard and answered by the Father.

"But you, dear friends, build yourselves up in your most holy faith and pray in the Holy Spirit." (Jude 20 NIV)

We are told to pray in the Holy Spirit to receive power to build our faith to believe and live our lives according to God's will, which is the last aspect of the Holy Spirit's power in our transformational process.

Power to live according to God's will

The Apostle Paul says in Galatians 5:24-25, "And those who are Christ's have crucified the flesh with its passions and desires. If we live in the Spirit, let us also walk in the Spirit."

The Holy Spirit gives us the power to live in the will of God. The only problem is our natural desires also want a say in this process.

"Walk in the Spirit and you shall not fulfill the lust of the flesh. For the flesh lusts against the Spirit, and the Spirit against the flesh; and these are contrary to one another, so that you do not do the things that you wish." (Galatians 5:16-17)

To win this battle we must put to death the passions and desires that war with the Holy Spirit. The only way we can do this is to take them to the cross of Christ and crucify them daily. In other words, put them to death every day.

This is at the heart of Jesus command for all who are on this journey to spiritual transformation.

"If anyone desires to come after Me, let him deny himself, and take up his cross daily, and follow Me." (Luke 9:23)

The only power strong enough to accomplish this is the power of the Holy Spirit residing within.

Getting filled to overflowing

How do we receive the filling of the Holy Spirit? How can we overflow with His power?

It all starts when we come to believe in Jesus Christ as the Apostle Paul said to the church in Corinth.

"Do you not know that your body is the temple of the Holy Spirit who is in you, whom you have from God, and you are not your own? For you were bought at a price; therefore glorify God in your body and in your spirit, which are God's." (1 Corinthians 6:19-20)

Jesus paid the price with His life on the cross.

When we come into the saving knowledge of Jesus Christ, what Jesus Himself described as being born again, John 3:3, then our spirit becomes the dwelling place for the Holy Spirit. It's at this time we are filled but not necessarily overflowing.

We see this in the life of the disciples. After Jesus' death, burial, and resurrection, He appeared to them in His glorified body.

"Peace to you! As the Father has sent Me, I also send you." (John 20:21)

Jesus sent them out into the world, but not alone.

"Receive the Holy Spirit." (John 20:22)

Yet this wasn't the complete filling. There was more to come. Not just once but over and over again from Jesus.

"Behold, I send the Promise of My Father upon you; but tarry in the city of Jerusalem until you are endued with power from on high." (Luke 24:49)

Endue means to endow or provide completely with a quality or ability. Jesus is saying He wanted them to be clothed completely in Holy Spirit power.

"For John truly baptized with water, but you shall be baptized with the Holy Spirit not many days from now." (Acts 1:5)

Jesus makes it clear there's another filling, an additional anointing of the Holy Spirit referred to as the baptism of the Holy Spirit where they would receive His power.

Using the word baptism means to be completely immersed.

It's as if the Lord is saying, "I want to completely immerse you in the Holy Spirit so His power will overflow every area of your life."

"But you shall receive power when the Holy Spirit has come upon you. You shall be witnesses to Me in Jerusalem and in all Judea and Samaria and to the end of the earth." (Acts 1:8)

As they gathered on the Day of Pentecost when the Holy Spirit filled and overflowed them, there was a sound from heaven like a mighty rushing wind. There appeared tongues of fire hovering over each one, and they were filled with the Holy Spirit and began to speak in languages they didn't know, but languages known to those who were listening. (Acts 2:1-6)

What we often fail to notice is that they had already been filled with the Holy Spirit when they first believed. Right after the resurrection Jesus breathed on them saying, "Receive the Holy Spirit." While they were filled, they weren't overflowing. This came later at the Day of Pentecost through what Jesus called the Baptism of the Holy Spirit.

From biblical testimony we can see this doesn't always happen the same way because the Holy Spirit will do it any way He wants.

We see both the filling and overflowing happening simultaneously at the house of Cornelius. As the Apostle Peter was proclaiming the gospel message the Holy Spirit fell upon them and, like the disciples at Pentecost, they began speaking in tongues and magnifying God. (Acts 10)

When Phillip went to Samaria to proclaim the gospel they came to believe and were water baptized. When the apostles in Jerusalem heard of the great work that was going on, they sent Peter and John to Samaria. The Samaritans were believers who had only been baptized with water, but not with the Holy Spirit, so Peter and John laid hands upon them to receive the Holy Spirit, Acts 8.

Throughout the life of the church the disciples received additional fillings to empower them, such as when they were praying after being warned by the Jewish authority not to speak any more in the name of Jesus. The house was shaken and they were filled with the Holy Spirit. Acts 4:31.

The reason we need the continual filling and overflowing power of the Holy Spirit is because without it, these steps and transformational principles won't work. We're trying to put spiritual principles into practice using natural techniques.

In Galatians 3:3 the Apostle Paul said, "Are you so foolish? Having begun in the Spirit, are you now being made perfect by the flesh?"

Without the Holy Spirit, all we're doing by putting these biblical principles into practice is conforming ourselves to other's expectations. This isn't true transformation. Transformation isn't an outward-in work. Instead it is a work that begins inside and manifests itself to the outside world.

We cannot be effective without the filling and overflowing power of the Holy Spirit. It's a necessity if we're going to live an effective godly life in an ungodly world. It's a necessity if we're going to regain that fire and make a difference for Christ in our lives, in our families, and in our communities.

How can we receive the empowering presence of the Holy Spirit once we come into the faith of Jesus Christ?

Wait!

There have been plenty of formulas when it comes to receiving the baptism of the Holy Spirit. But as we have seen there is no one set way. The best advice is to follow Jesus' instruction to pray and wait, Luke 24:49.

Jesus told His disciples to go and wait in Jerusalem until they received the power and baptism of the Holy Spirit. They didn't wait by doing nothing. Waiting isn't a passive noun; it's an active verb. Waiting is an action we take.

Consider those who serve in restaurants. They are called waiters. They don't wait for us to serve them; rather they wait by serving us. And so we are to wait upon the Lord in our service to Him, and the way we serve the Lord is by serving one another.

"When did we feed you, give you drink, take you in, clothe you, or visit you in prison or when you were sick?" Jesus was asked.

"Assuredly, I say to you, inasmuch as you did it to one of the least of these My brethren, you did it to Me," He replied in Matthew 25:40.

As the disciple's waited as Jesus told them to do, they prayed and were unified in their prayer. As they prayed, the Holy Spirit descended and filled them to overflowing with the power of God to be witnesses.

There's power in waiting.

"But those who wait on the Lord shall renew their strength. They shall mount up with wings like eagles, they shall run and not be weary, and they shall walk and not faint." (Isaiah 40:31)

Like the disciples, we too need to wait, but not by doing nothing, rather we are to wait with great expectation and anticipation for the Holy Spirit to move and clothe us in His power, for the baptism of the Holy Spirit.

Ask

"So I say to you, ask, and it will be given to you; seek, and you will find; knock, and it will be opened to you. For everyone who asks receives, and he who seeks finds, and to him who knocks it will be opened." (Luke 11:9-10)

What's interesting is that we should be continually "asking," "seeking," and "knocking."

Jesus said that if we being evil know how to give good gifts to our children, how much more will He give unto us the gift of the Holy Spirit when we ask, Luke 11:13.

Today, we all should ask the Lord to give us the Holy Spirit. Don't doubt because the Father and Son want to give to us the Holy Spirit without measure, fully and completely so we can be His church, His bride, and His witnesses.

Conclusion

Without the indwelling power of the Holy Spirit, we won't be able to effectively live this life for the Lord. Today ask the Lord for the baptism of the Holy Spirit and wait with expectation and anticipation for God to fulfill His promise.

In John's gospel, Jesus said that while Satan comes to steal, kill and destroy, He had come for the exact opposite, to give abundant life.

"The thief does not come except to steal, and to kill, and to destroy. I have come that they may have life, and that they may have it more abundantly." (John 10:10)

Jesus has indeed given us eternal life, but He also gives us an abundant overflowing life this side of eternity. To avail ourselves of His abundance we need the baptism of the Holy Spirit. We need to be filled to overflowing.

Reflection and Discussion

1. Is there an area of ministry or in your life where you feel defeated? What do you need more of God's power for?

2. Have you asked the Holy Spirit to fill you so you can have His power to overcome in these areas? In what ways are you waiting for the Holy Spirit's filling?

3. Have you asked God for the Baptism of the Holy Spirit? What is your testimony of being filled and baptized?

4. How has the Holy Spirit's filling helped you in the past? In the book of Revelation it says they overcame the devil by the "word of their testimony." (Revelation 12:11)

5. In what ways are you stopping the move of the Holy Spirit in your life? Read again Galatians 5:16-17. What can you do to prevent the lust of the flesh from winning the battle within?

6. What one thing will you take away from this chapter and apply to your life?

Chapter Eight

Surrendered and Submitted

When a police officer yells, "Put your hands up," you can be pretty sure he isn't telling you to praise the Lord. Instead he's telling you to surrender. Lifting hands into the air universally means to surrender, which makes sense when we do it in church. We are surrendering all of who we are, including our praise, to the Lord.

In the old television crime drama, "Dragnet," Jack Webb, the actor who played police sergeant Joe Friday, would tell informants to provide, "Just the facts."

So here are the facts concerning our need to surrender and submit our lives to the Lord.

There is no transformation without surrender and submission. On this journey toward spiritual transformation if we haven't surrendered to the Lord's word, will, and way, how can we say we know God? Instead, it makes us windbags, full of hot air.

Knowing God's Word doesn't mean we know God. Just because we may know some passages in the Bible doesn't mean we know God. There are many who know the Bible better than many Christians, but don't believe in the God of the Bible.

There are people from other religions who know right from wrong. They are moral individuals and support moral values but they skip the Lord who inspires those values. They know what the Bible says about right and wrong, but they don't know the Lord God of the Bible.

Knowing God's will isn't always an indicator of belief. We must do the will of God. This is exactly what the Apostle Paul explains to us. He talks about those who call themselves Jews, who believe in God and follow His word. They believe they are spiritual guides to the blind and teachers of the foolish. But instead they missed it by violating the very things they say are wrong. In Matthew 23:24 Jesus called them "blind guides."

As a Christian it's time to stop talking a good game and start getting into the game. If we know what God's Word says, it's time we started doing it. Stop "saying" we love God, and truly love Him by doing what He says.

The Lord gives an appropriate description of many who occupy church pews.

"My people come to you, as they usually do and sit before you to listen to your words, but they do not put them into practice. With their mouths they express devotion but their hearts are greedy for unjust gain. Indeed, to them you are nothing more than one who sings love songs with a beautiful voice and plays an instrument well, for they hear your words but do not put them into practice." (Ezekiel 33:31-32 NIV)

Jesus described the surrendered life.

"If anyone desires to come after Me, let him deny himself, and take up his cross daily, and follow Me." (Luke 9:23)

A surrendered life is a life lived in accordance to the cross of Jesus. It's a cross life. It is a life lived in submission to our Creator.

The best illustration of this type of life is found in the life of clay in the hands of a potter.

"But now, O Lord, You are our Father; we are the clay, and You our potter; and all we are the work of Your hand." (Isaiah 64:8)

The clay has given up its right to be whatever it wants in order to be what is in the mind and heart of the potter. Isaiah is saying we are the clay, and the Lord is the potter. As clay we have given up our right to be whatever we want. We are surrendered and submitted to the will of God and His design and shape for our life.

"And the vessel that he made of clay was marred in the hand of the potter; so he made it again into another vessel, as it seemed good to the potter to make." (Jeremiah 18:4)

A surrendered and submitted life says, "Lord, You have the right to make me whatever You want to make me, and to put me wherever You want to put me." It's having a heart totally surrendered to God and submitted to His will.

If a surrendered and submitted life is key to our spiritual transformation, what are those things that hinder the process?

Pride

The root of rebellion is pride. This was the very first sin because it was the sin of Satan and all sin originates in him.

"Your (Satan's) heart was lifted up because of your beauty; you corrupted your wisdom for the sake of your splendor." (Ezekiel 28:17a)

"How you are fallen from heaven, O Lucifer, son of the morning! How you are cut down to the ground, you who weakened the nations! For you have said in your heart: 'I will ascend into heaven, I will exalt my throne above the stars of God; I will also sit on the mount of the congregation on the farthest sides of the north; I will ascend above the heights of the clouds, I will be like the Most High.' Yet you shall be brought down to Sheol, to the lowest depths of the Pit." (Isaiah 14:12-15)

Pride was the original sin. It led to Satan's discontent with where the Lord placed him, even though he was the highest of all created beings. Pride got the best of Satan because he wanted more, he wanted to be like God, which is exactly what he tempted Adam and Eve with in the garden.

"Then the serpent said to the woman, 'You will not surely die. For God knows that in the day you eat of it your eyes will be opened, and you will be like God, knowing good and evil.'" (Genesis 3:5)

Pride is acting as if we don't need God. Pride says we can do God's work without God. Pride is deadly to our spiritual growth and hinders our relationship with God. Pride literally makes God our adversary.

In Leviticus 26:19 the Lord said, "I will break the pride of your power; I will make your heavens like iron and your earth like bronze."

In the end it's all about being humble. Our spiritual transformation comes through humility not pride.

"God resists the proud, but gives grace to the humble." (James 4:6)

Self-sufficiency

The second thing hindering our surrender and submission to God is being self-sufficient or self-reliant.

Making ourselves the center of our own universe usually leads to regret and disappointment.

An adage warns, "Don't let your mouth write a check your body can't cash."

How often do we hear someone talk about how great they are? But with all the talk of greatness we often see later some sort of struggle, like a debilitating disease or a struggle just to make ends meet.

Self-sufficiency is failure to recognize the uncertainty of life! Life can vanish at any time! We can't depend on ourselves or even others. Instead we are completely dependent upon God's grace for life!

In Proverbs 3:5-6 Solomon says, "Trust in the Lord with all your heart and lean not on your own understanding; in all your ways acknowledge Him, and He shall direct your paths."

When we make our plans for today and for the future, we need to take time to acknowledge God's rule and sovereignty, and when our plans go south, we won't be disappointed. We'll be content following God's lead looking forward to another great adventure with Him.

"You do not know what will happen tomorrow. For what is your life? It is even a vapor that appears for a little time and then vanishes away. Instead you ought to say, 'If the Lord wills, we shall live and do this or that.'" (James 4:14-15)

The church at Laodicea, often considered the Last Days Church, best illustrates the dangers of being self-sufficient. To this self-sufficient church Jesus said in Revelation 3:17, "You say, 'I am rich, have become wealthy, and have need of nothing'--and do not know that you are wretched, miserable, poor, blind, and naked."

Church members thought they could do it all because they had it all. They thought they could do church without God. In the end, however, they had no real power to change who they were. All their stuff couldn't transform them. Their self-sufficient attitude failed them miserably.

This brings me to the third thing that hinders our surrender and submission to God.

Materialism

Wealth and possessions bring pride. The Lord shared this lesson with the Israelites.

"When your herds and flocks grow large and your silver and gold increase and all you have is multiplied, then your heart will become proud and you will forget the Lord your God." (Deuteronomy 8:13-14a NIV)

The richer you become and the more possessions you acquire, the harder it will be to surrender them to the Lord and follow Him. This was the case concerning the rich young ruler who asked Jesus what it took to inherit eternal life.

"Good teacher, what good thing shall I do that I may have eternal life?" (Matthew 19:16)

Jesus said to this young man that he lacked just one thing, and to get it he had to sell all he had and give it to the poor and then come follow Him. But the young man left sorrowful because he possessed a lot of things, more than he was willing to surrender, and in the end missed out on an amazing transformational opportunity.

In Matthew 19:24 Jesus said, "It is easier for a camel to go through the eye of a needle than for a rich man to enter the kingdom of God."

We must realize whatever is in our pockets today will most likely end up in someone else's tomorrow. All we long for, all we desire will end up being lost, and in the end, burned.

When we finally get what we desire, we soon find that it doesn't bring the satisfaction we expected, especially when a bill follows in the mail.

In the book of Revelation the Lord reveals the end of humanity's obsession over getting more possessions.

"The fruit that your soul longed for has gone from you, and all the things which are rich and splendid have gone from you, and you shall find them no more at all … (They) cried out when they saw the smoke of her burning." (Revelation 18:14, 18a)

Let's not allow the cares of the world and the deceitfulness of riches choke out God's transformation.

Religion

It's amazing to listen to people who are wrapped up in their religion, or even in their denomination. They think theirs is the only way, boasting and reveling in their perceived knowledge. The Apostle Paul tackles this in Romans chapter two.

"Indeed you are called a Jew, and rest on the law, and make your boast in God, and know His will, and approve the things that are excellent, being instructed out of the law, and are confident that you yourself are a guide to the blind, a light to those who are in darkness, an instructor of the foolish, a teacher of babes, having the form of knowledge and truth in the law." (Romans 2:17-20)

They were boastful and glorying in their religious affiliation. But God isn't interested or impressed with our religions, Christian or otherwise.

In Romans 10:2-3 the Apostle Paul says, "For I bear them witness that they have a zeal for God, but not according to knowledge. For they being ignorant of God's righteousness, and seeking to establish their own righteousness, have not submitted to the righteousness of God."

God isn't interested in man's religions. He is interested in our lives. God wants us to be living for Him, not just talking about how good our church's worship services are, or how large or grand our churches may be.

Religion cannot transform anyone. It may make people morally better, but nothing made by man can transform. Only the Lord God living inside can transform. It's all about a relationship with Jesus Christ, not in a professed religion. This is the judgment that'll be rendered when people think otherwise.

"Many will say to Me in that day, 'Lord, Lord, have we not prophesied in Your name, cast out demons in Your name, and done many wonders in Your name?' And then I will declare to them, 'I never knew you; depart from Me, you who practice lawlessness.'" (Matthew 7:22-23)

Negative connotation

Pride, self-sufficiency, materialism, and religion have hindered living a surrendered life. The main deterrent to living a fully surrendered life, however, is the negative connotation that comes with the word, "surrender." Yet even so, there are several positive aspects to surrender that make living a surrendered life attractive.

Freedom

We cannot be truly free until we are fully surrendered.

That's a confusing statement because people view surrender as a loss of freedom. Being able to lay down the burden of having to get our own way is extremely freeing, however. One of the greatest human bondages is trying to get what we want rather than accepting what we already have.

Whenever the idea of surrender comes up we think about it in terms of losing our personal freedom. But true freedom comes from surrender, because we've freed ourselves from the prison cell of our own needs and desires.

In 1 Peter 2:18 the Apostle Peter said, "Slaves, submit yourselves to your masters with all respect."

This seems like strange advice. Of course slaves are to submit to their masters, that's what slaves do. But Peter said it's possible to obey without having a spirit of submission. Outwardly we may be obeying the Lord, but inwardly we're still in rebellion and the prison of our circumstances.

Service

Surrender and service go hand in hand. They cannot be separated, because we can't be surrendered to the Lord and not be involved in His service. There is no such thing as a living sacrifice that doesn't surrender everything in the Lord's service.

When an animal was sacrificed, the whole animal was used, not just a couple of parts. A sacrifice was all or nothing. We can't say we want to surrender only this part of our lives to the Lord. With the Lord it's all or nothing.

In Romans 12:1b the Apostle Paul said, "Present your bodies a living sacrifice, holy, acceptable to God, which is your reasonable service."

Many Christians can easily quote this but few are doing it. Becoming a living sacrifice means picking up the cross and following Jesus no matter where He leads. It means dying to self and living for the Lord. It means living a surrendered life, a submitted life, a cross life.

This was the type of life Jesus lived. The greatest example was when Jesus took up the towel and washed the disciple's feet. Jesus took upon Himself the lowest position of a slave, and yet He was Lord.

"For I have given you an example that you should do as I have done to you. Most assuredly, I say to you, a servant is not greater than his master nor is he who is sent greater than he who sent him." (John 13:15-16)

Jesus not only died on the cross, He lived with the cross fully in view, He lived a cross life, which was a life of service to the very ones He created. There is no transformation without surrender. If a surrendered and submitted life is key to spiritual transformation, how do you go about living a surrendered and submitted life?

Cast cares upon the Lord

The Apostle Peter said surrender begins with humbling ourselves under the mighty hand of God. When the time is right, God will exalt and transform us. Peter explained this.

"Casting all your care upon Him, for He cares for you." (1 Peter 5:7)

To cast means to throw, but within the context of the word there's no indication of going and picking it back up. It's a once-and-forever tossing our cares and worries upon the Lord.

Peter probably had in mind the words Jesus spoke.

"Come to Me, all you who labor and are heavy laden and I will give you rest. Take My yoke upon you and learn from Me, for I am gentle and lowly in heart and you will find rest for your souls. For My yoke is easy and My burden is light." (Matthew 11:28-30)

Jesus added more.

"Therefore I say to you, do not worry about your life, what you will eat or what you will drink, nor about your body, what you will put on ... For your heavenly Father knows that you need all these things. But seek first the kingdom of God and His righteousness and all these things shall be added to you." (Matthew 6:25a; 32b-33)

We cast our cares upon the Lord because He cares for us. We must surrender all anxieties, worries, cares and concerns to the Lord and leave them with Him. Surrender everything over to the Lord, because He knows what we truly need.

Lay aside the weights

"Let us lay aside every weight and the sin that so easily ensnares us." (Hebrews 12:1b)

Weights are not the same as sins. The writer of Hebrews makes delineation between the two. So what is a weight if not sin?

Weights are those things that keep us from fully following after God. They may be things like the Internet, TV, or recreational activities. These things are not wrong, but when we spend more time with them than with the Lord they can hinder our spiritual growth.

So we are to surrender them but not gently. "Lay aside" means a violent taking off of those things that hinder, snare, and trip us up on this journey toward spiritual transformation.

If you were drowning and your clothing was dragging you to the bottom, you'd tear them off so you could swim to the top. This is what the writer of Hebrews is getting at when He tells us to lay asides these weights.

Conclusion

So "who" or "what" do we need to be surrendered and submitted to? The "who" is the Lord God, and the "what" is His word.

Surrender to Jesus as the master of your life. Submit to Him your heart, soul, mind, and strength. Don't worry about tomorrow.

Tomorrow has a whole new set of worries, according Matthew 6:24. We must surrender and submit our lives to God today.

We have a choice. We can carry the world on our shoulders like Atlas, straining under its weight, or we can give ourselves wholly over to the Lord and let Him carry us in the palm of His hand.

Maybe we've tried to surrender in the past only to find the process tiresome and inconvenient. But we must surrender anyway. Whatever we are holding onto we must give it over to Jesus. It's time to lay aside every weight and the sin that is tripping us up, and cast all our cares and worries unto the Lord. It's time to surrender our lives and be free from everything that is keeping us from fully following after Jesus, and from being fully transformed into His image.

Reflection and Discussion

1. What area of God's Word have you been neglectful about following? What does God's Word say about it? What specific steps can you take to start changing your direction and begin to follow God?

2. What areas of pride, self-sufficiency, materialism, and religion have you allowed in your life that has hindered your following God? Remember all have sinned and fallen short of God's glorious standards for life (Romans 3:23)

3. What positive things come from being fully submitted and surrendered to the Lord?

4. Is there any area in your life that you're holding back in your service of the Lord? Has God given you a gift or talent that you're not actively using? How are you living the "cross life?"

5. What are those weights dragging you down? What are those things that while they may not be sinful are keeping you from fully following God?

6. What one thing will you take away from this chapter and apply to your life?

Chapter Nine

Agents of Change

We've come to that point in our journey where we have to look at the process of change. But what are we to change? Better yet, what or who are we to change into?

Change for change sake isn't always best. Instead, change needs a goal and there is no greater goal than being like Jesus Christ, our Creator. Not only did Jesus create the world and everything in it, John 1:1-3, but He also created us, not only as human beings but as believers as well.

In 1 Corinthians 5:17 the Apostle Paul said, "If anyone is in Christ, he is a new creation. Old things have passed away; behold, all things have become new."

Jesus Christ is our physical and spiritual creator. Therefore our goal is to be changed more and more into His image every day and in every way. This was God's ultimate purpose for us.

"For those God foreknew, He also predestined to be conformed to the likeness of his Son." (Romans 8:29a NIV)

God's plan and purpose is for us to be like Jesus Christ. This should be our highest goal and aspiration. Our goal is to change and be more like Him.

To help in this process there's an "agent of change" available.

An agent of change is someone who gives us the necessary tools and supplies the necessary motivation for change to take place.

By the very definition the agent of change is the Holy Spirit as the Apostle Paul explains.

"But we all, with unveiled face, beholding as in a mirror the glory of the Lord, are being transformed into the same image from glory to glory, just as by the Spirit of the Lord." (2 Corinthians 3:18)

The Holy Spirit is continually transforming us into the image of our Lord Jesus Christ. While we were created in the image and likeness of God at the creation described in Genesis 1:26, that image was tarnished and stained when sin entered the picture. When we become born again we become new creations in Christ being transformed back into that original image, which was on full display when Jesus walked this earth.

Further, since the Holy Spirit is Lord and our agent of change, He will accomplish this change, this transformation work, the way He sees fit and which bests fits our situation. The way He most often transforms us is through a set of tools known as spiritual disciplines.

Spiritual disciplines are those principles that help facilitate spiritual growth enabling us to move forward in this journey toward spiritual transformation and spiritual maturity. It is the spiritual disciplines that help keep us on that straight and narrow road leading to heaven.

There may be many disciplines and subsets to each discipline but here is a list of the more popular including the consumption of God's Word, prayer, worship, evangelism, fasting, confession, meditation, solitude, submission, service, and stewardship.

It's important to know what these disciplines are, how they operate, and how to incorporate them in our lives, but knowing and doing are two different things.

"To know the mechanics does not mean that we are practicing the disciplines. The spiritual disciplines are an inward and spiritual reality, and the inner attitude of the heart is far more crucial than the mechanics for coming into the reality of the spiritual life," said Richard Foster.[3]

The Apostle James stated it far more succinctly.

"Be doers of the word, and not hearers only, deceiving yourselves." (James 1:22)

The Holy Spirit uses all these disciplines, but there are three through which He does His greatest work. We can think of these as a hammer, screwdriver, and wrench in a toolbox, or the spoon, fork, and knife in a silverware drawer. The main three used by the Holy Spirit are prophesy, prayer, and praise.

Tool 1: Prophecy

Prophecy refers to either foretelling future events or forth-telling God's Word through preaching and teaching. Here it simply means the Word of God, and involves making God's Word a part of our daily lives.

"All scripture is God-breathed and is useful for teaching, rebuking, correcting, and training in righteousness, so that the man of God may be thoroughly equipped for every good work." (2 Timothy 3:16-17 NIV)

The fact it is God-breathed means God the Holy Spirit authored it. God's Word equips everyone with everything they need to live an effective life for God. Literally, the Bible is transformational and transformative. It is God's answers and directions for life in a world filled with sin.

---

[3] Richard Foster, Celebration Of Discipline: The Path to Spiritual Growth, 1978, Harper and Row, New York New York, pg. 3

A standard statement of faith would be that the Bible is fully inspired by God and is without error in its original manuscript. It's the infallible rule of Christian faith and practice. It is incapable of being wrong or mistaken.

The key is that it's God's Word and not just another religious book. Therefore it's useful, that is, it's practical, beneficial, and relevant.

"No spiritual discipline is more important than the intake of God's Word. Nothing can substitute for it. There is simply no healthy Christian life apart from a diet of the milk and meat of God's Word," Donald Whitney wrote in "Spiritual Disciplines for the Christian Life."[4]

Since the Word of God seems to be the number one tool used by the Holy Spirit to bring about spiritual transformation, what can we do to further the process?

The answer is to approach the Bible from every angle using our senses, our mind, and spirit.

Hearing God's Word

Jesus doesn't downplay the importance of listening to God's Word being preached or taught. In the early days that's primarily how learning occurred. Jesus tells us when we take time to hear God's Word being taught there's a blessing attached.

"Blessed are those who hear the word of God and keep it." (Luke 11:28)

There is a blessing attached to hearing God's Word spoken or taught, but we also need to obey what we're hearing, and this occurs through faith as the Apostle Paul tells us.

---

[4] Donald Whitney, Spiritual Disciplines for the Christian Life, 1991, Navpress, Colorado Springs, CO, pg. 24

"Faith comes by hearing, and hearing by the word of God." (Romans 10:17)

We need faith for our salvation and sanctification -- being transformed and living for Christ -- that comes from hearing the Bible's message.

In Romans 10:14 Paul said: "How then shall they call on Him in whom they have not believed? And how shall they believe in Him of whom they have not heard? And how shall they hear without a preacher?"

There's great importance attached to hearing God's Word being spoken and taught, but it's important to understand that we're hearing someone else's digested food. It's what God has revealed to the teacher or preacher and they regurgitate it for more general consumption.

Here are a couple of practical suggestions to hear God's Word.

- Attend worship services and Bible studies where God's Word is being taught, and
- Listen to teaching via electronic media while in your car or at home.

Reading God's Word

Jesus expects us to read and know God's Word. Several times He asked, "Have you not read?" assuming those who claim to be God's people would at least read His word.

"Blessed is he who reads and those who hear the words of this prophecy, and keep those things which are written in it; for the time is near." (Revelation 1:3)

We need to stop being a stranger to God's Word and start becoming close friends with it. God has a blessing for us, not just when we read and hear the prophecy of Revelation, but when we hear and read the whole of His word, the Bible.

It's allowing God's Word to be our BFF (best friend forever) and to be such a friend means we spend quality and quantity time with it.

Every day we face problems and temptations where we need God's help, instructions, guidance, and encouragement. So every day we need to read God's Word to get His take on how to live this life in a world gone haywire. Reading the Bible is instrumental in shaping our view of the world, or our worldview.

Some practical suggestions include:

- Find regular time to read the Bible every day;
- Carry a pen and paper to write what the Lord is saying to you;
- Find a Bible reading plan and follow it, and
- Pick a verse or phrase the Lord speaks to you about and meditate on it.

Studying God's Word

Hearing and reading God's Word can provide us with a general overview of his plans for us, however by studying God's Word we can discover its depth for our lives.

The Bible describes the scribe Ezra, not only as a student of God's Word, but as a teacher as well.

"Ezra had determined to study and obey the law of the Lord and to teach those laws and regulations to the people of Israel." (Ezra 7:10 NLT)

Hopefully by this point all of us have noticed a common denominator with all three disciplines. That is obedience. We must listen and obey, read and obey, and study and obey.

Most people are intimidated when it comes to the study of God's Word. They feel inadequate. But the study of God's Word is quite simple, and most Bible study tools are available on the Internet. All it takes is a little time and determination, along with pad of paper and pen.

Practical suggestions include:

- To go deeper, to find out more of what God's Word says, use what is available, from cross references to concordances found in your Bible.

- Use the Internet Bible resource centers for many tools that can be of benefit.

- General Bible study aides include a Concordance, Bible Encyclopedia, and a Greek and Hebrew word study, and

- Take time to sit with your pastor or a Bible teacher to learn how to effectively use these resources.

Reverence for God's Word

There is one last point in this whole process that's essential. You might say it's what makes the other three work. It is our reverence for God's Word.

We need to approach God's Word with both awe and reverence, along with an attentive mind and teachable heart. We need to be thankful for God's revelation in all its fullness and simplicity for the great truths it unfolds, and the counsels it contains.

There needs to be a reverence for God's Word, and to show such reverence you need to prepare your heart to effectively consume it. There needs to be a sincere seeking after God. Such reverence is shown from the Jewish people. It says that when Ezra opened the book in the sight of all the people, they all stood up, which was a sign of reverence, Nehemiah 8:5.

To show such reverence today, pray before you listen, read, or study God's Word. Ask the Holy Spirit to open those things He wants you to learn and that will help you in the transformational process.

Look at God's promise.

"He will be gracious if you ask for help. He will respond instantly to the sound of your cries." (Isaiah 30:19 NLT)

This leads to the second discipline or tool in the Holy Spirit's toolbox.

Tool 2: Prayer

Years ago a movie starring Jodie Foster called "Contact" was released. Foster's character was listening to find some sort of signal or message from outer space. The place where she hung out in this pursuit was New Mexico's VLA (very large array). It consists of 27 huge radio antennas and is one of the world's premier astronomical radio observatories.

Isn't it interesting the lengths to which people will go and how much money they're willing to spend just to get a message from heaven? Yet God has clearly spoken to us through His Son, Jesus Christ, and through His word, the Bible. God is also interested in hearing from us and doesn't make us jump through hoops or pay money to do so.

King David said, "O You who hear prayer." (Psalm 65:2 NIV)

Jesus promised not only would He hear us, but He will answer as well.

"Ask and it will be given to you; seek, and you will find; knock, and it will be opened to you. For everyone who asks receives, he who seeks finds, and to him who knocks it will be opened." (Matthew 7:7-8)

Just as Jesus expects us to read God's Word, He also expects us to pray. He also told his disciples to always pray.

In his letters, the Apostle Paul echoed the same message.

In Colossians 4:2 Paul said, "Continue earnestly in prayer, being vigilant in it."

We must be diligent and make prayer and integral part of our lives. To the church in Thessalonica the Apostle Paul tells us to "Pray without ceasing." (1 Thessalonians 5:17)

God expects us to devote ourselves to prayer, which is our communication with God. It is an open line where we speak with God and allow God to speak to us.

Nobody questions the need for prayer, but we may question why prayer is so difficult and how can we pray without ceasing?

To answer the second part of that question, to pray without ceasing means to always be aware of our need of God's assistance and guidance. It's to be in an attitude of prayer, paying attention to God no matter what we're doing and not leaving God outside during life's interruptions.

Prayer often is difficult because we simply don't believe it works. When Herod saw how killing the Apostle James pleased the Jewish leaders, he arrested the Apostle Peter intending to put him to death as well. So the church gathered and prayed.

Before the day of Peter's execution, an angel delivered him from his prison cell. Peter made his way to the church where the members were praying for him. When he knocked at the gate, instead jumping for joy at God's answered prayer, the congregation refused to acknowledge it, Acts 12:12-16.

Many don't pray because they don't believe God hears them. If you find yourself in this category take to heart what it says in Hebrews that the way to heaven is open and the Lord hears your prayers.

"Let us therefore come boldly to the throne of grace, that we may obtain mercy and find grace to help in time of need." (Hebrews 4:14)

"Boldly" means "with all speech." God opened the way through His Son Jesus that whoever believes in Him can now have direct access to heaven's throne.

Practical suggestions include:

- Make prayer a habit. Pray constantly and consistently.

- Don't be haphazard in your prayers. Don't allow your prayer life to be all over the place or interrupted. The Bible in 2 Corinthians 10:5 says to bring every thought into captivity to the obedience of Christ, and

- Don't be hypocritical in your prayers. Don't just pray when you know someone else is watching. Jesus said in Matthew 6:6 to go into that secret place to pray.

Tool 3: Praise

"Oh come, let us worship and bow down; let us kneel before the Lord our Maker." (Psalm 95:6)

Someone said, "Man worships his work, works at his play, and plays at his worship."

This describes our worship more than many of us would like to admit. We come to a worship service, where the Lord is the one we have gathered to honor, only to half-heartedly sing of His worthiness. We then leave thinking we've done something great for God.

"These people draw near to Me with their mouth and honor Me with their lips, but their heart is far from Me. And in vain they worship Me." (Matthew 15:8-9a)

The word worship comes from an Anglo-Saxon word pronounced "worthship." It means God is worthy of our love and adoration. He is worthy of all the honor we can muster and then some. We can see this in what the angels and saints say in heaven.

"You are worthy, O Lord, to receive glory and honor and power; for You created all things, and by Your will they exist and were created ... Worthy is the Lamb who was slain to receive power and riches and wisdom, and strength and honor and glory and blessing." (Revelation 4:11; 5:12)

We can worship like this by focusing on Him, by reading His word, and finding out just who and how great and marvelous He is. Only then will we have a greater appreciation of His worth. The more we comprehend what God is like, the more we'll worship Him.

When we gather with other believers in worship we need to have our focus where it belongs; on God and not on others, or on the football game coming up on TV, or what's for lunch. When we're not fully engaged, we're not really worshiping. This applies not only to our singing songs of praise and worship, but also when God's Word is being read or taught we need to be thinking of how it applies to our life.

"But the hour is coming, and now is, when the true worshipers will worship the Father in spirit and truth; for the Father is seeking such to worship Him. God is Spirit, and those who worship Him must worship in spirit and truth." (John 4:23-24)

Before this can take place, we must have the Holy Spirit within, or as He is called in John 14:17, "the Spirit of truth." Without the Holy Spirit there is no true worship happening. It's the Holy Spirit, the Spirit of truth, who motivates and inspires worship, and who better since He is the third person of the Godhead.

It is the Holy Spirit who brings us into the saving knowledge of Jesus Christ and who reveals the fullness of God through the truth of His Word. Worship is our way of showing God how much we love Him by truly honoring Him both within and without the walls of the church.

Conclusion

Since our ultimate goal is to be changed more and more into the image of Jesus Christ, we should start today by giving our agent of change, the Holy Spirit, full range in our lives. We need to allow the Holy Spirit full access to our heart, our mind, and our spirit, allowing Him to transform us through the various spiritual disciplines; most notably the disciplines of prophesy, prayer, and praise.

Reflection and Discussion

1. In what way are you allowing God's Word to transform you? What are some of the ways you can allow God's Word to transform you?

2. What is keeping you away from daily getting into God's Word? What can you do in order to spend more time with the Lord in His word?

3. How is your prayer time with the Lord? Are you just requesting from God what you want, or are you taking time to allow God to speak to you? In your time of prayer what specifically has God been saying?

4. Describe your worship of the Lord? How do you worship God?

5. Take time and look at the spiritual disciplines of witnessing, fasting, meditation, solitude, service, and stewardship. How can you implement these to make a difference for the Lord in your life?

6. What one thing will you take away from this chapter and apply to your life?

CHAPTER TEN

BEING AND STAYING ON-PURPOSE

We're on one of the most exciting journeys we'll ever take, a journey to spiritual transformation. An exciting part of the journey is learning to be and stay on-purpose,[5] which, in turn, helps us continue the journey toward spiritual maturity.

The journey won't be easy; in fact it'll be difficult, even painful at times. Finding our purpose, finding what God created us to be, is beyond price. It's priceless.

When people have a purpose in life they enjoy everything they do a whole lot more, even the hard and inconvenient stuff.

Unfortunately, many believers' lives are more like a random string of events reacting to whatever's happening around them. They either have no control or they've lost control. It's called the tyranny of the urgent. It's where the daily circumstances of life control us instead of God and His Word.

They wonder, "What's become of my dreams?" and become increasingly resentful and impatient with everything and everybody. Outside they may look like the picture of health and vitality, but inside they're

---

[5] Kevin W. McCarthy, The On-Purpose Person: Making Your Life Make Sense, 1992, Pinon Press, Colorado Springs, CO.

slowly dying. They're not sure if they even know what they want and as a result are living unfulfilled lives, lives without goals, lives without purpose.

They feel like they're just marking time and time is running out. They feel their life is falling apart with only a frayed piece of twine holding it all together. They don't know how much longer they can keep up the façade. They've become a shell of their former selves, losing the man or woman God created them to be.

Where did it go wrong? How can they get back in touch with what's truly important?

My brother escaped these thoughts through alcohol, drinking more and more until he became addicted. Instead of reaching out for help, he withdrew into his own protective cocoon losing hope by the minute until he finally took his own life.

Others try gimmicks and programs. They try goal-setting programs, seminars, and lectures. They'll read a book or listen to a CD. They try everything and anything, but their lives continue spinning out of control. It may stop for a while, but they haven't fixed the problem. Their despair and disappointment with life picks up speed when they find that all the methods the world promotes doesn't work.

And then it hits them and they ask, "Where is God in all of this?"

This is not a bad place to be, because it's when we begin to look to God that answers follow and hope arises.

What's needed is purpose. We need to become on-purpose believers. We need to understand we have only so much time on earth to make a difference, or as our church's purpose statement reads, "Making a difference in our community for Christ."

Think of it this way, a light bulb's purpose is to shine. When it isn't shining it isn't living up to what it was created to be. But when we turn the light on it brings a wonderful glow to those in need, those in darkness. We might say a light bulb that is shining is on-purpose.

Being on-purpose requires discipline and perseverance, which is why so many people remain off-purpose. They'd rather sit in the pews hoping to slide into heaven on a wing and a prayer.

But God has a divine design in mind for His people, one that is unique for each individual.

We can't look to others for our purpose. We can't sit with a counselor or coach and have them tell us what our purpose is. We have to search it out through time in reflection, God's Word, and prayer. A gift analysis helps, but it doesn't tell you how to use God's gifts and talents.

When we find our purpose it'll bring joy and energy into our lives.

How do we get started? How do we find meaning and purpose for our lives? How can we get on this path of becoming an on-purpose believer?

Many of the seminars and books I mentioned earlier try to help people find their purpose by asking what they want. They talk about various areas of life and explain how people need to define their wants and desires, like where they want to be financially, vocationally, professionally, relationally, and spiritually. They talk about being physically, socially, mentally, and spiritually healthy. While these things are all good and necessary, they've missed the key ingredient for it all to work, God.

Having a personal relationship with God is key to being on-purpose, because God is the one who created and designed us for His purpose and glory. This is what the Lord showed the prophet Jeremiah.

"Before I formed you in the womb I knew you; before you were born I sanctified you; I ordained you a prophet to the nations." (Jeremiah 1:5)

The Apostle Paul confirms this in a his letter to the Philippian Church saying, "For it is God who works in you to will and to act according to his good purpose." (Philippians 2:13 NIV)

In Ephesians 2:10 the Apostle Paul says, "For we are His workmanship, created in Christ Jesus for good works, which God prepared beforehand that we should walk in them."

While we may see this reality, we still have questions to which we need answers. "Being a child of God is all well and good, but I still want to have all that other stuff. I still need a job. I still need my health. I still want a family to share my life with. I still need food and clothing. What about all that?"

Jesus provides the answer.

"Seek first the kingdom of God and His righteousness, and all these things shall be added to you." (Matthew 6:33)

Jesus said not to worry about all the other stuff and instructs us to focus on our relationship with God. He said that God would give us what we need without all the hassle and stress that goes along with it.

Our journey begins when we accept Jesus Christ as our Savior and Lord and start upon the narrow road.

Good versus best

As we travel on this journey, one of the first things we must determine is what's good versus what's best.

Consider Moses. He may have believed living in Midian, being a husband and father, and tending to his father-in-law's flocks was a good life. But God gave him another task that best fit the purpose God had designed him for. That meant returning to Egypt and leading God's flock, the Israelites, out of bondage.

Many ask that if we're content with where we are in life, isn't that the place God has designed for us?

At this point, we must get brutally honest about what we're going to do in life for the Lord. There are a lot of good things in which to get involved, but just because they may be good doesn't mean they are the best.

Maybe the job you have is good. But is that job the best for you and God? Does your work meet the criteria of fulfilling God's purpose for your life?

This doesn't mean we should quit our jobs and become missionaries. However, maybe we should be looking down the road for a job that fits God's unique design for us, where we'll feel fulfilled.

The same goes for ministerial work. There are a lot of good things that need to get done in the ministry. However, the place in which we may find ourselves in the ministry may not necessarily be the best place we can be for God. I'm not advocating leaving a ministry high and dry, but maybe we should start looking elsewhere for a better fit and accept how God has made us unique for the ministry.

Some of us may be sitting and doing nothing because we don't know or can't hear God's calling. While we wait, however, we can volunteer to serve in any number of areas within our church and community. Those who wait upon the Lord are those who are serving Him. As previously discussed, waiting is not passive; rather it's active.

Jesus encouraged service from all believers.

"...whoever desires to become great among you, let him be your servant. And whoever desires to be first among you, let him be your slave--just as the Son of Man did not come to be served, but to serve, and to give His life a ransom for many." (Matthew 20:26b-28)

No matter what we do, we must remember we've been called to make a difference for Christ within our spheres of influence. We're called to be the light shining in the darkness. Remember, light is only fulfilling its purpose when it's on.

Do right things the right way

The second thing to determine is our need to do right things the right way.

We should think about our daily routines as we ask if we're doing what's consistent with God's purpose for our lives. If you were to put a percentage of time on what you do, how much of your day would you say is on-purpose?

To do right things the right way takes dedication and perseverance. It requires determination on our part to find out the right thing and do it the right way for God, as opposed to a way that may be quicker or easier.

When we're doing things just to get by, then not only are we unproductive, but we're also not being on-purpose.

Further, doing right things the right way doesn't change the circumstances of life. It changes the way we respond to these circumstances.

Since my brother's suicide, I have found myself more frustrated and angry at what he did, not only to himself but also to his family. How he has negatively affected my life and family.

What I have come to realize is my need to turn the frustration and anger into forgiveness. I need to turn the negative into a positive and stay on-purpose.

In the disciple's prayer Jesus said that if we want to stay on purpose then we need to forgive those who have sinned against us, Matthew 6:12.

Practical suggestions

We should all start a time sheet listing what we do and the time we spend doing it. It's possible to later generalize this, but we should see how it plays out first. The time we list should include how much is spent at work and how much of that time is productive. Include how much time is spent in activities with family and friends, and in exercise and recreation. It's vital that we be completely and brutally honest.

Now look at how much time is allocated to the Lord. Not only in coming to church but also in time spent in God's Word, prayer, and talking with others about the Lord. Does it come out to around 16 hours a week? This represents giving to the Lord a tithe of our time.

During this evaluation we'll find out if we're actually stealing time, not only from the Lord, but also from family, employers, and ourselves.

Now write down what an ideal day looks like when we're living on-purpose. List what we consider important areas of our lives, and compare it to a normal day. We then ask ourselves have we been more on-purpose or off-purpose?

In this whole process keep the Lord front and center, because the Bible in Proverbs 14:12 and 16:25 says that while our ways or plans fall short, God's ways are perfect and right.

"Commit your way to the Lord, trust also in Him and He shall bring it to pass." (Psalm 37:5)

Remember God is the one who ordains our ways, which means it isn't our plan or purpose at all; rather it's the Lord's so we need to do it right. Do the right thing the right way.

Make an investment

The final step in this whole process of being and staying on-purpose is to make an investment with both time and resources.

"Do not lay up for yourselves treasures on earth, where moth and rust destroy and where thieves break in and steal. But lay up for yourselves treasures in heaven, where neither moth nor rust destroys and where thieves do not break in and steal. For where your treasure is, there your heart will be also." (Matthew 6:19-21)

If our lives seem off kilter and bankrupt, maybe we're making the wrong investments. Instead we should intentionally make an investment in God's kingdom. Intentionally invest in what matters most and stop wasting time and energy on the nonessentials, the things of the world.

Today the hot topic is all about multi-tasking. The only problem with multi-tasking is our minds aren't built to handle that sort of life for long. It's one of the major causes of stress and burnout. Instead we should do one thing and do it well and then move to the next. When a thought or idea comes along, write it down on a sheet of paper. This way you'll remember it when the time comes for it to be taken care of.

Now take a moment and ask, "Where should I invest my time and resources?"

Practical suggestions

We must take time with God. We must ask, "If time is money, am I earning interest on what I am investing my time in, or am I paying interest on the time I spend?"

We can tell the difference by determining if what we're doing is time consuming and tiring, or energizing and refreshing. If we find ourselves dreading every day we need to start realigning our day toward God and His purpose.

We should start when we first get out of bed. Take time to pray asking God to give us wisdom to live on-purpose. We must take time to worship and read God's Word; get aligned with God before the day begins and we'll be more on-purpose throughout the day.

This was King David's practice.

"Give ear to my words, O Lord, consider my meditation. Give heed to the voice of my cry, my King and my God, for to You I will pray. My voice You shall hear in the morning, O Lord; in the morning I will direct it to You, and I will look up." (Psalm 5:1-3)

Throughout the day

- Take time when you go into a store to greet someone, give a smile and encouragement to those who help you.

- Take time to give an encouraging word to your fellow workers and your boss. Take time to listen to what they're going through and pray for them.

- Take time to say hello to your neighbor, a friend, or even a total stranger, and

- Take time and share the love of Jesus with those you meet throughout the day.

Now many of us may be saying, "I don't have enough time in the day."

If that's the case, prune back and cut away those things that are not a good fit or are not producing the fruit of the Spirit in your life. The fruit of the Spirit is love, joy, peace, patience, kindness, goodness, faithfulness, gentleness, and self-control, Galatians 5:22-23.

In addition to time, we also need to invest our resources. It's known as the tithe. It's a requirement of every believer as outlined in God's Word. Even in the New Testament Jesus said it should be adhered to while not forgetting the weightier matters of the law including justice, mercy, and faith, Matthew 23:23.

It isn't about the amount, although to tithe generally means 10 percent. It's far more involved. It involves having a joyful heart. God says He loves a cheerful giver, 2 Corinthians 9:7.

Our giving also needs to be intentional and proportional with God's purpose for our lives.

Remember it's all about having an attitude of gratitude.

God has given us the ability to earn a living and if we're not tithing on what we earn, then this needs to be addressed. Does our giving line up with God's Word and purpose? We can't expect God's help and provision if we're not willing to follow His Word and do it His way.

If we're barely making ends meet, we should rearrange our budgets so we can start giving. Maybe all we can give right now is 2 or 3 percent. That's okay as long as we are working toward 10 percent. We can start by cutting back on questionable purchases. We shouldn't buy Starbucks when we can brew our own and flavor it to our liking.

Recently we purchased a single serving coffee maker for only a few dollars. It was a great deal. The only problem is the pre-packaged one-cup servings are expensive. So we bought some reusable-serving dispensers to put our own coffee into. Now a cup of coffee cost pennies, instead of a dollar or more.

Start using your talents, that is, those abilities God has given you. Use them to further His kingdom and not just your own. Remember God isn't as interested in your ability as He is in your availability.

Write a purpose statement

Begin writing a purpose statement. This is key! A purpose statement is a statement of why God has us here on earth. God has chosen us for a specific purpose. As a result He expects us to succeed in that purpose.

Our vision and mission comes from our purpose statement. That's why it's so important.

To write a purpose statement we first ask ourselves:

- What does living on-purpose for God look like in my life?
- What are my most important values?
- What do I want my future to look like?
- What are my priorities?
- What do I want as my legacy? What do I want written on my gravestone?

Conclusion

If life seems to make no sense, we should find our purpose. God has uniquely created all of us. We are God's divine design created for His kingdom purposes. When we start figuring out our purpose we'll start having hope for the future and a direction for the present.

Some questions to ask include:

- Do we feel on or off purpose?
- What did we do today that felt on-purpose, and what did it feel like when we missed it?
- What actions are we choosing to implement to find and stay on purpose?
- Are we giving God our time, resources, and talents?

- Are we giving with a joyful heart, and in accordance with God's Word?

- Who can we share God's story of grace too, and are we willing to share it?

Remember the purpose of light is to shine. Being on-purpose for God is sharing the one message He's given, and by the way, it isn't called the Great Commission for nothing.

Reflection and Discussion

1. What is God's calling for your life? If you don't know, then what has God gifted you with? What sort of time have you spent thinking and pondering this question?

2. While there are a lot of good things you can be doing for God, what is the best thing? How can you parlay those things that you're doing into doing what's best?

3. Are you opting only to do enough to get by? How are you doing the right thing the right way? How much of your time are you on-purpose for God?

4. In what ways are you investing in God's kingdom? Where are you investing your time and resources, and where should you be investing them?

5. This week how did you invest your time for God? What sort of fruit for God's kingdom did it produce? How was it in accordance with God's Word?

6. What one thing will you take away from this chapter and apply to your life?

Chapter Eleven

Pursuing God's Presence

Over the years I've realized an important truth. The Lord desires our presence. He's so desirous for our presence He promises His presence in return. The Lord is so passionate about this He willingly lowered Himself to our level to become a human being.

In Philippians 2:6-8 the Apostle Paul writes of Jesus, "Who, being in the form of God, did not consider it robbery to be equal with God, but made Himself of no reputation, taking the form of a bondservant, and coming in the likeness of men? And being found in appearance as a man, He humbled Himself and became obedient to the point of death, even the death of the cross."

Jesus revealed His desire of maintaining this relationship after His death and resurrection.

"And lo, I am with you always, even to the end of the age." (Matthew 28:20a)

This was how it was in the beginning. God was so desirous for an intimate relationship with His creation, man, that every day He would walk the Garden of Eden with Adam. But that intimacy was broken when sin entered, and sin's awful outcome was that Adam and Eve hid themselves from the Lord's presence.

Imagine that.

Here are Adam and Eve hiding from the Lord who had created and abundantly blessed them. But God wasn't going to have any of such nonsense.

"Where are you?" God called.

How tragic. Adam and Eve were willing to identify more with their sin than with the Lord and as a result, avoided the Lord's presence. They hid themselves hoping God would leave them alone. But God did the opposite. He pursued them.

Did you catch that? God was pursuing them.

We try to hide ourselves from God but God pursues us so we can have a life-changing personal encounter and relationship with Him.

This was played out in Jacob's life in Bethel, which means "the house of God." Jacob was running for his life to escape the wrath of his brother Esau, whom he had cheated to gain Esau's birthright and inheritance.

Jacob was on his way to his Uncle Laban's house to escape Esau and find a bride. On his way he stayed in a nondescript place where God revealed His presence in a dream. In the dream Jacob saw a ladder reaching from earth to heaven with angels ascending and descending upon it. (Genesis 28:12)

The Lord spoke to Jacob promising him land along with "descendants as numerous as the dust upon the earth." (Genesis 28:14 NLT)

It was the same covenant God had made with Jacob's father, Isaac, and grandfather, Abraham.

The only problem was that Jacob never had a relationship with God. We see this as Jacob's story continues to unfold. And Jacob never changed, he continued to be deceitful, but God didn't let that stop Him from pursuing Jacob.

God placed Jacob in a situation that absolutely required his undivided attention, with a need to seek God's presence like never before.

Jacob was returning home when he learned his brother Esau was coming to greet him with 400 men of war. Jacob left his family on one side of the river Jabok and crossed to the other side to seek God's presence. There he wrestled with the very real and physical presence of the Lord, Genesis 32:24.

God allows these types of situations to happen in our lives to force us to fully seek His presence. God wants to do a new work within us to change us and to make us more like His Son, Jesus Christ.

God desires our presence; not to harm us, but to help us through a life filled with turmoil and strife. That's why we should never want to go anywhere if the presence of the Lord isn't going with us.

Moses felt the same way when he refused to travel until he had the Lord's assurance He was going with him.

"My presence will go with you, and I will give you rest," the Lord told Moses in Exodus 33:14.

Moses responded, "If Your presence does not go with us, do not bring us up from here." (Exodus 33:1)

The prophet Isaiah gives us advice.

"Seek the Lord while He may be found, call upon Him while He is near." (Isaiah 55:6)

It was this very promise and presence that took me from the church I pastored in Las Vegas to Mesquite, Nevada.

More than a year before moving to Mesquite, the Lord told us to bring our church, Hallelujah Christian Fellowship, under a denominational covering. After much prayer and speaking to several different denominations, we chose The Foursquare Church because it was the closest match to who God made us to be.

Not long afterward I went on a sabbatical. During this time I heard the Lord say through His word, "You can go back to the church if you want, but My presence isn't going to be there for you anymore."

That's all I needed to hear, and God made sure I got the message saying, "Once you put your hand to the plow, if you look back you'll never draw a straight line for Me again."

I immediately contacted the head of our district and it wasn't long before I was in Mesquite, Nevada, taking over Living Waters Fellowship.

Unfortunately, not many of us want this kind of an encounter because of our sin, or maybe because we've grown accustomed to living without God's personal presence, His personal touch in our lives.

We've become comfortable coasting along in our Christianity. We're afraid of the change that'll occur once we have a close encounter of the God kind, because we like our sin and our present way of life too much.

This doesn't change God's desire for our presence, however, nor does it change His promise to give His presence to those who seek Him.

In Joshua 1:9 the Lord said to Joshua, "Have I not commanded you? Be strong and of good courage; do not be afraid, nor be dismayed, for the Lord your God is with you wherever you go."

God promises if we do what He commands and not be afraid of the outcome or the problems we'll encounter along the way, He'll be with us on this journey to spiritual transformation, with an eternity in heaven at its end.

It is the same promise given by King David in the Shepherd's Song.

"Yea, though I walk through the valley of the shadow of death, I will fear no evil; for You are with me; Your rod and Your staff, they comfort me … and I will dwell in the house of the Lord forever." (Psalm 23:4, 6b)

No matter how deep or dark the problems may be, even if it's the darkness of death, God will always be there, and His presence will comfort us through it all.

Corrie Ten Boom, who survived the Holocaust said, "There is no pit so deep, that God's love is not deeper still."

King David also knew of God's protection and deliverance that accompanies His presence.

"The angel of the Lord encamps all around those who fear Him, and delivers them." (Psalm 34:7)

The Lord is with His people to deliver, protect, and provide for their needs.

God longs to be close to His people, and He's so passionate in this pursuit He gave His Son, Jesus Christ, to die in our place for our sins. Through this selfless act of love God makes it possible for us to be in His presence, now and for all eternity.

What's sad is that many people live all their lives never experiencing this intimacy with God. They've never lived in the presence of the Lord, who is Creator of heaven and earth. Instead they're caught up in the trappings of the church, as well as the business and busyness of life.

But God's plan and desire is that we seek and pursue His presence as much as He seeks and pursues ours.

The Athenians were always on the lookout for the existence of spiritual entities and the Apostle Paul told the people of Athens that God was very close.

"They should seek the Lord in the hope that they might grope for Him and find Him, though He is not far from each one of us; for in Him we live and move and have our being." (Acts 17:27-28a)

How amazing is that? If we would search for God, even if we're blind and groping along the way, we'll find Him.

God is within reaching distance, never far from us. We don't have to go to great lengths to find God, nor do we have to make a holy journey. We don't even have to belong to a religion or denomination to find God.

God is within reaching distance. He's close to everyone who seeks Him. Just reach out and there He is. That's God's promise, plan, and desire.

Yet, as close as He is, God never forces His attention or presence upon us. Yes, He pursues us by placing all types of situations in our paths to get us to turn back and seek Him, but He'll never force us.

Rather, God calls out to us. He woos us in an attempt to encourage us to reach out to Him, much as He did in the Garden of Eden with Adam and Eve. But the decision is still ours to make. God is patiently waiting for us to seek His presence.

To pursue means to continue to persevere until the desired goal is achieved. So don't quit. God's blessings are just waiting.

"Indeed we count them blessed who endure. You have heard of the perseverance of Job and seen the end intended by the Lord--that the Lord is very compassionate and merciful." (James 5:11)

Pursuing God's Presence

Pursuing God is serious business and requires all the time and energy we can muster.

"Seek the Lord and His strength; seek His face evermore." (Psalm 105:4)

This pursuit needs to be a continual effort on our part, because it's not a temporary relationship we're entering. It isn't a once a week, Sunday morning church meeting type of relationship God desires, but a daily walk with Him from the moment we wake to the time we sleep.

We've entered a marriage relationship with God. Our pursuit needs to be passionate. We see this passion in the Great Commandment where we're told to love the Lord with all our heart, soul, mind, and strength, Deuteronomy 6:5; Mark 12:30.

In Deuteronomy 4:29 the Lord said, "But from there you will seek the Lord your God, and you will find Him if you seek Him with all your heart and with all your soul."

Put whatever effort necessary to seek and pursue this relationship with God. It's such a pursuit God desires from all who come to Him.

Many think they're too busy with life, work, kids, or whatever to pursue God with such a passion. If this is the case, know that when our desire is for God's presence, only then will we be in the middle of God's plan and purpose for our lives.

So let's open our eyes and see what God is doing and join in.

Trust God and move with Him. The elders of Israel did the same.

"When you see the ark of the covenant of the Lord your God, and the priests, the Levites, bearing it, then you shall set out from your place and go after it." (Joshua 3:3)

The ark was the visible representation of God to His people.

God gave the same advice to the children of Israel in their wilderness experience. When the pillar of cloud and fire, the presence of the Lord, would lift off the tabernacle and move, the children of Israel were to move with it.

So, when we see the Lord move, we must not wait for an engraved invitation, or for some sign from heaven, instead we must move and experience God's presence right now.

"My presence will go with you, and I will give you rest." (Exodus 33:1)

Remember God's promise.

"Trust in the Lord with all your heart, and lean not on your own understanding; in all your ways acknowledge Him, and He shall direct your paths." (Proverbs 3:5-6)

Let's put into practice God's presence by passionately pursuing Him, by going to those places where His presence dwells.

Practical suggestions

To passionately pursue the presence of God, a good place to start and to maintain this relationship is going to those places where His presence is found. There are many such places to help us along in the journey including:

a. The Word of God (the Bible)

"All scripture is given by inspiration of God. It is profitable for doctrine, for reproof, for correction, for instruction in righteousness, that the man of God may be complete, thoroughly equipped for every good work." (2 Timothy 3:16-17)

The Apostle Paul said everything written in the Bible is inspired, or more literally "breathed out" by the Lord God. It isn't a book written by man but by the Lord who inspired men to record the words for our benefit.

"Knowing this first, that no prophecy of Scripture is of any private interpretation, for prophecy never came by the will of man, but holy men of God spoke as they were moved by the Holy Spirit." (2 Peter 1:20-21)

b. Prayer

"Let us therefore come boldly to the throne of grace, that we may obtain mercy and find grace to help in time of need." (Hebrews 4:16)

Boldly in Greek means with all speech. Therefore, our prayers transport us to God's heavenly throne room.

The Apostle Paul in Philippians 4:6-7 said, "Be anxious for nothing, but in everything by prayer and supplication, with thanksgiving, let your requests be made known to God; and the peace of God, which surpasses all understanding, will guard your hearts and minds through Christ Jesus."

c. Evangelism

"Go therefore and make disciples of all the nations, baptizing them in the name of the Father and of the Son and of the Holy Spirit, teaching them to observe all things that I have commanded you; and lo, I am with you always, even to the end of the age." (Matthew 28: 19-20)

Jesus promised, "I am with you always," when we are actively engaged in the Great Commission.

d. Service

"'For I was hungry and you gave Me food; I was thirsty and you gave Me drink; I was a stranger and you took Me in; I was naked and you clothed Me; I was sick and you visited Me; I was in prison and you came to Me.' Then the righteous will answer Him, saying, 'Lord, when did we see You hungry and feed You, or thirsty and give You drink? When did we see You a stranger and take You in, or naked and clothe You? Or when did we see You sick, or in prison, and come to You?' And the King will answer and say to them, 'Assuredly, I say to you, inasmuch as you did it to one of the least of these My brethren, you did it to Me.'" (Matthew 25:35-40)

When we serve others we are actually serving Jesus. This is also a part of the Great Commandment. We show our love for God, loving Him with the whole of our being, by loving our neighbors as ourselves, Mark 12:30-31.

e. Fellowship

"For where two or three are gathered together in My name, I am there in the midst of them." (Matthew 18:20)

When we enter church we are entering into the Lord's presence.

We see the Lord's presence at the inception of the church. As the believers were gathered in one place seeking the presence of the Lord, the Holy Spirit descends and fills the place.

"When the Day of Pentecost had fully come, they were all with one accord in one place. And suddenly there came a sound from heaven, as of a rushing mighty wind, and it filled the whole house where they were sitting. Then there appeared to them divided tongues, as of fire, and one sat upon each of them. And they were all filled with the Holy Spirit and began to speak with other tongues, as the Spirit gave them utterance." (Acts 2:1-4)

Conclusion

Seek the Lord while He may be found. Passionately pursue His presence, and not only will He be found, but will bless your efforts.

"Call to me and I will answer you and tell you great and unsearchable things you do not know." (Jeremiah 33:3 NIV)

REFLECTION AND DISCUSSION

1. How have you been running away from God? Have you been identifying with your sin more than with the Lord? What has God been doing in pursuit of having that relationship with you?

2. How much are you willing to give to pursue God's presence in your life?

3. In what ways has the busyness of life kept you away from having time with the Lord?

4. Where can you go to find God's presence for your life? What's keeping you from doing these things?

5. In what ways have you found God ministering to you as you have been ministering to others on behalf of God?

6. What one thing will you take away from this chapter and apply to your life?

Chapter Twelve

Potholes that Damage Transformation

As we travel on this journey to spiritual transformation, we're going to find potholes along the way designed by Satan to break us down and stop our progress. Along the way the Lord also places speed bumps to slow us down so we won't go too fast and miss a turn, which are those lessons God wants us to learn.

Our journey to heaven requires traveling a road of faith because our faith in God allows Him to direct our steps giving us guidance along the way. Solomon states this beautifully.

"Trust in the Lord with all your heart, and lean not on your own understanding; in all your ways acknowledge Him, and He shall direct your paths." (Proverbs 3:5-6)

We need guidance because there are curves, hills, and valleys along the way, and if we're not careful we'll run right off the road. There are also potholes from the stress of living that are so faith jarring they can cause major breakdowns.

We need to hear God's voice as we travel on the way prepared by Him.

"Prepare the way for the Lord; make straight in the wilderness a highway for our God. Every valley shall be raised up, every mountain and hill made low; the rough ground shall become level, the rugged places a plain. And the glory of the LORD will be revealed." (Isaiah 40:3-5a NIV)

In this chapter I'll share some of the potholes to spiritual transformation. In Chapter 13 we'll look at some God-installed speed bumps that purposely slow us down so we don't miss His lessons.

Potholes to spiritual transformation

We really don't have to drive far or wait very long before the first pothole. They are formed by road fatigue where cracks in the pavement from stress expand allowing chunks of pavement to become loose.

If unattended these potholes can grow to several feet in width and length. While they are usually only inches deep they can become large enough to damage tires and a vehicle's suspension. Further, serious accidents are directly attributed to these menaces.

There are many potholes on this journey to spiritual transformation, but four are the most prevalent. These can damage your ability to continue toward spiritual transformation.

Consumer mindset

Consumer Christians are believers in Jesus Christ who conduct their own form of spirituality. They attend church only for what it offers them.

A man visited us in Las Vegas to ask about our church and its statement of faith. He then asked a question that took me by surprise.

"What can your church do for me?" he asked.

My answer caught him off guard as well.

"Probably not what you're expecting," I replied. "We'll tell you of your need to make Jesus Christ first in your life."

Church isn't about meeting a need. Church is about introducing people to God, giving glory to Jesus Christ, and serving the kingdom of God, rather than being served.

Jesus put the kibosh on consumer mentality.

"But he who is greatest among you shall be your servant." (Matthew 23:11)

"The Son of Man did not come to be served, but to serve." (Matthew 20:28)

Consumer mentality has taken people away from the church because the church doesn't fit their idea of what it should be or the type of church they want. But you cannot live a Christian life and travel on this road separated from the life of the church.

I've heard people say, "I don't need church."

They're wrong.

Speaking of the church as the body of Christ, the Apostle Paul, in 1 Corinthians 12:14-15, said, "For in fact the body is not one member but many. If the foot should say, 'Because I am not a hand, I am not of the body,' is it therefore not of the body?"

The church doesn't exist for the member; the member exists for the whole. We need each other. When we go to church and if the church doesn't have what we want, God doesn't tell us to go to another church. He instructs us to stay and provide what others require.

When we think we can live without the church we're in danger. When it comes to receiving help in time of need, we'll be like the people of Laish. They dwelt in peace and security without ties to anyone. They wrongly thought they were self-sufficient.

When the tribe of Dan came upon them they were destroyed.

"There was no deliverer because it was far from Sidon, and they had no ties with anyone." (Judges 18:28)

I often hear people say they get their spiritual food from watching their favorite pastors on TV. When they're in trouble, however, who do they reach out to for help? They reach out to the local church for help, prayers, and support although they offer nothing in return. They soon return to their TVs once the crisis is over.

I had a family member who loved me but never came to church. Instead my family member sat in front of the TV every Sunday morning watching their favorite preacher. One day I got a call from that relative asking for help.

"Why not just call the TV preacher for help?" I asked.

"That's not practical," I was told.

They didn't get my sarcasm.

Christians need to stop this consumer mentality that has not only destroyed the church, but is a pothole in their journey toward spiritual transformation.

Materialistic mindset

Materialism is the desire for more and it's a dangerous and destructive trap.

In 1 Timothy 6:9 the Apostle Paul said, "But those who desire to be rich fall into temptation and a snare, and into many foolish and harmful lusts which drown men in destruction and perdition."

Jesus taught several parables concerning the materialistic mindset

The parable of the rich fool

"Teacher," said someone listening to Jesus one day, "tell my brother to divide the inheritance with me."

Jesus replied with a parable.

A farmer had a great harvest. It was so great his barn wasn't big enough to hold it all. So he decided to tear it down and build a bigger one.

God told him, "You fool! This very night your life will be demanded from you. Then who will get what you have prepared for yourself? This is how it will be with anyone who stores up things for himself but is not rich toward God." (Luke 12:20-21 NIV)

The moral of the story!

"Watch out! Be on your guard against all kinds of greed. A man's life does not consist in the abundance of his possessions." (Luke 12:15)

The rich man and the beggar

This is a story of a rich man and a beggar named Lazarus. The rich man lived a life of luxury. At his gate sat Lazarus who wished for nothing more than to eat the crumbs from the rich man's table.

Both men died and while Lazarus went to Abraham's bosom, the rich man ended up in hell. In his agony the rich man asked Abraham to send Lazarus over with a drop of water to cool his parched mouth. Abraham reminded him of the past.

"Son, remember that in your lifetime you received your good things, while Lazarus received bad things, but now he is comforted here and you are in agony." (Luke 16:25 NIV)

The moral of the story!

We can't take it with us so give to those who are in need. When we do, we are giving it directly to Jesus.

"Assuredly, I say to you, inasmuch as you did it to one of the least of these My brethren, you did it to Me," said Jesus in Matthew 25:40.

The rich young ruler

A rich young man came to Jesus asking what he could do to inherit eternal life.

After affirming the man kept the commandments, in Matthew 19:21, Jesus said: "If you want to be perfect, go, sell your possessions, and give to the poor, and you will have treasure in heaven. Then come, follow me."

At hearing Jesus' words the young man departed sadly because "he had great wealth." (Matthew 19:22)

The moral of this story!

Jesus said, "It is easier for a camel to go through the eye of a needle than for a rich man to enter the kingdom of God." (Matthew 19:24)

Money itself isn't bad or evil but it can become a problem. Money can cause people to fall into traps of temptations.

"For the love of money is a root of all kinds of evil, for which some have strayed from the faith in their greediness, and pierced themselves through with many sorrows." (1 Timothy 6:10)

The love of money is the problem. People do all sorts of bad things to make money including lying, slander, stealing, prostitution, murder, dealing drugs, and the rest. It may also cause believers to wander from the faith, leave the church, or turn away from God because money becomes their god.

When people have a materialistic mindset they'll stop at nothing to get as much as they can, including compromising their beliefs.

"No one can serve two masters. Either he will hate the one and love the other, or he will be devoted to the one and despise the other. You cannot serve both God and money." (Matthew 6:24)

What is the Bible's prescription for the materialistic mindset?

Jesus said, "Do not store up for yourselves treasures on earth ... But store up for yourselves treasures in heaven where moth and rust do not destroy and where thieves do not break in and steal. For where your treasure is, there your heart will be also." (Matthew 6:19-21 NIV)

In 1 Timothy 6:7-8 the Apostle Paul said, "For we brought nothing into this world, and it is certain we can carry nothing out. And having food and clothing, with these we shall be content."

Works mindset

One of the basic tenants of the Christian faith is that good works won't save anyone. Works are important but they can actually be potholes waiting to do damage.

The Apostle Paul took time through his letters to make this known, especially his letter to the church in Rome.

"Therefore, we conclude that a man is justified by faith apart from the deeds of the law." (Romans 3:28)

Humanity did not create itself, nor can humanity save itself. All humanity did was to lose itself. There is nothing we can do to make ourselves righteous in the eyes of a holy and righteous God outside of believing in what He did for us.

The Apostle Paul said in Romans 3:23, "For all have sinned and fall short of the glory of God."

You are justified and made righteous by faith alone in what God did by sending His Son, Jesus Christ, to die for our sins. The Apostle Paul said as much to the church in Ephesus, even though God created us for good works.

"For by grace you have been saved through faith, and that not of yourselves; it is the gift of God, not of works, lest anyone should boast. For we are His workmanship, created in Christ Jesus for good works, which God prepared beforehand that we should walk in them." (Ephesian 2:8-10)

It isn't by chance the Apostle Paul writes this to the church in Ephesus. The church was founded upon his preaching. It was on fire for God, racing throughout Asia Minor with the gospel message. But it hit some potholes and veered off its true course. So some repair work had to be done to get back on the road toward spiritual transformation.

Jesus, too, spoke to the Ephesian church.

"I know your works, your labor, your patience, ... and you have persevered and have patience, and have labored for My name's sake and have not become weary." (Revelation 2:2-3)

If the Lord had stopped there they could have patted themselves on the back and continued on as if nothing were wrong or out of place. They would have felt good about themselves. But Jesus isn't finished because good works, too, are potholes on the road to spiritual transformation.

The church in Ephesus was doing great things for God and God commended it. In the process, however, church members were losing the most important thing, their first love relationship with God.

Please understand our best is never going to be good enough when we leave God out of the picture; when we make religion the end all rather than having what He desires most, a personal relationship with Him.

As Jesus explains, the church had the form of religion, but lost its passion for God in the process.

"Nevertheless, I have this against you, that you have left your first love," Jesus said in Revelation 2:4.

Jesus is actually telling the church, "It just isn't the same between us anymore."

That's what happens when we replace a relationship with God with good works or religiosity. When Jesus is no longer at the center of our hearts, our spiritual transformation, our becoming more like Christ takes a serious hit. The pothole of good works has damaged our ability to move forward.

So Jesus gives the church in Ephesus and to us, the tools to repair the potholes and get back on the right path, to get back to that first love relationship.

"Remember, therefore, from where you have fallen; repent and do the first works." (Revelation 2:5a)

The problem with the Ephesian church wasn't in its doctrine about God, but in its devotion to God.

Most churches are caught up doing good works. Most are involved in doing good things for its members, its community, and others around the world.

But it isn't the works that should be drawing people; rather it should be our love for Jesus, which is evident by the things we do.

Religious mindset

I remember seeing the golden headpiece of King Tutankhamen, known familiarly as King Tut. It was a beautiful death mask of the young king. What got my attention were the lengths taken to keep the dead king safe. What the archeologists found in his tomb was something similar to Russian nesting dolls.

First was the large sarcophagus made from a single block of quartzite. Under the lid, which weighed well over a ton, archeologists found a golden effigy of the king atop a gilded wooden coffin. Once the heavy lid was removed, a third coffin, made entirely of gold was discovered. Inside that coffin were the mummified remains of King Tut with a golden ceremonial mask covering his head and shoulders.

Only after all the elaborate outward decorations were finally removed were archeologists able to reveal what lay beneath, a 3,000-year-old preserved dead guy.

Jesus likened our spirituality and religious mindset to Tut's final resting place.

In Matthew's gospel, Jesus spoke to religious leaders about the traditions, rules, and regulations they place on others while they follow another path of self-promotion and aggrandizement.

"Woe to you, scribes and Pharisees, hypocrites! For you are like whitewashed tombs which indeed appear beautiful outwardly but inside are full of dead men's bones and all uncleanness." (Matthew 23:27)

Religious people go to extreme lengths to keep alive the traditions of their religion, even to their detriment. Those who cover themselves with religious traditions are usually trying to hide dead spirituality.

Jesus didn't come to establish a religion, however, with all its religious trappings. He came to establish a personal intimate relationship with us.

This is what differentiates the two. Religion is an end in itself. It makes traditions and rules equal to a personal relationship with God. But Jesus said a relationship with God boils down to two basic things, loving Him with the whole of our being, and loving our neighbors as ourselves.

Religion has taken what God made so simple and attainable into intractable and unattainable rules and regulations, leaving the Great Commandment in its wake.

In Mark 7:8 Jesus said of these traditions, "For laying aside the commandment of God, you hold the tradition of men."

Jesus saw the religious mindset turning people away from God rather than moving them closer. He makes it clear it isn't what's on the outside that matters; it isn't all about rules and traditions. It's all about what's on the inside. It's all about a living faith in Jesus.

In our world today there are a multitude of options when it comes to religions among them are Islam, Judaism, Buddhism, Hinduism, Mormonism, Scientology, Christian Science, New Age, and more. There is also Christianity with its two main divisions, Catholicism and Protestantism.

Proponents of each tout their beliefs as exclusive, making the following rules and regulations everything in order to be considered worthy. They fail to promote the one thing that will truly make a difference, a personal relationship with Jesus Christ.

They are religious but lost. They are like King Tut's coffin, all nice and beautiful on the outside, but inside spiritually dried up and withered.

In 1 Timothy 3:5-7 the Apostle Paul summed up the religious mindset as those who are always learning but never coming to the truth; having the form of godliness but denying its unmistakable power.

Religion is dry and empty, void of life. Religion inspires and changes no one. Religions are places where there is little life, no passion, and a dead faith.

Instead of getting stuck in the pothole of a religious mindset, we must focus on Jesus Christ, away from the religious process.

Conclusion

Potholes in this journey to spiritual transformation are many and varied. Some are small while others are wide and deep. But they all slow and even stop our forward progress.

These include, but are not limited to emotions like fear, pride, along with the works of the flesh that the Apostle Paul identified as sin.

To move forward what's needed is timely and appropriate maintenance, which includes confession, repentance, and preventative measures like daily consuming God's Word, prayer, praise, and worship, along with the fellowship of other believers.

If we ignore these maintenance checks and preventative measures, these potholes will escalate geometrically.

Seal up these cracks so they don't turn into potholes. Confess them to the Lord and repent.

REFLECTION AND DISCUSSION

1. What are some of Satan's potholes you've found yourself falling into? How have they disabled your journey towards spiritual transformation?

2. What are your thoughts towards the local church? How has the consumer mindset dominated your thoughts and attitude towards the local church?

3. How have you compromised your faith for the sake of monetary gain? (Consider what you record on your taxes, or what you give the church in tithes and offerings)

4. What are you presently doing that's storing up treasures in heaven, and what are you doing that's getting you stuck in the pothole of materialism?

5. How have you replaced spending time with God with good works? How have the traditions and the trappings of the church gotten in the way of a personal relationship with Jesus Christ?

6. What one thing will you take away from this chapter and apply to your life?

Chapter Thirteen
God's Speed Bumps

As you travel on this journey to spiritual transformation, we're going to find potholes along the way designed by Satan to break us down and stop our progress. We saw some of these in Chapter 12.

In addition to Satan's potholes, the Lord places speed bumps in our way to slow us down so we don't go too fast and miss a turn or the lessons He's teaching us.

While Satan's potholes wreak havoc and accidently slow traffic, the Lord's speed bumps are intentionally designed to do just that. They are designed to slow our roll. Satan's potholes aren't the same as God's speed bumps. The difference is Satan's potholes are to be avoided, while God's speed bumps are meant to be experienced.

In traffic, speed bumps are effective methods for controlling vehicle speed. High visibility bumps and signage like, "Caution Speed Bump Ahead," are the best way to tell drivers to keep their speed at a minimum. It's important to pay attention because if you hit a speed bump going too fast vehicle damage can occur.

The Lord places speed bumps on our journey, along with sufficient signage found in His word to slow us down so we don't miss out on His promises and lessons. If we don't pay attention to these God-installed speed bumps, we just might damage our spiritual transformation.

Solomon tells us that we should give careful thought as to how we walk on this journey of faith.

"Watch the path of your feet and all your ways will be established." (Proverbs 4:26)

These speed bumps are found throughout the Bible in the lives of those we learn about in Sunday school. Jonah's speed bump was the whale. King David's speed bump was when Uzzah fell dead.

King David wanted to bring the Ark of the Covenant to Jerusalem. He unfortunately copied the Philistine's method of transport and put the ark on a cart. Along the way the oxen stumbled and Uzzah, the driver, put out his hand to prevent the ark from falling. The moment Uzzah's hand touched the ark he was struck dead. David was so upset he left the ark there and returned to Jerusalem.

Three months later, after repentance and researching God's Word, David returned. With the Levites carrying the ark as outlined in God's Word, the ark was restored to the tabernacle.

That is what speed bumps are designed to do. They make us regroup and reassess our situation in light of God and His word. They force us to slow down and ask, "Is this the right thing?"

Moses' speed bump was the burning bush.

After being exiled from Egypt, Moses was content with being a shepherd watching his father-in-laws flocks. He had a loving wife, Zipporah, and two sons, Gershom and Eliezer, whose names meant that while Moses was a stranger in a foreign land, God was helping him. Life was good.

But Moses wasn't living the life God had planned. So God placed a burning bush in his path. This was Moses' speed bump.

The rest of the story is history. Moses went back to Egypt and through God brought ten plagues upon the Egyptians forcing Israel's release, departure, and a meeting with God where His law was given along with the Promised Land.

Not all speed bumps, however, are whales or burning bushes. There are an infinite variety of spiritual speed bumps each uniquely designed by God to promote His plan and purpose for our lives. We just need to keep our spiritual senses open.

There are a wide variety of speed bumps, but there are a few common ones that have infinite possibilities.

Humility

What sends us over the edge more than anything else is pride, and so to slow our roll so we don't take a tumble the Lord humbles us.

"Pride goes before destruction and a haughty spirit before a fall." (Proverbs 16:18)

It's only when we're on our knees that we find it a lot harder to fall.

God used a talking donkey as a speed bump for Balaam. The story is found in Numbers 22.

The story unfolds when the Israelites camped on the plains of Moab as Moses was leading them to the Promised Land.

Balak, king of Moab, was afraid of the Israelites knowing what they had just done to the Amorites. So he sent for Balaam, a prophet and seer, and promised him a large sum of money if he would curse the Israelites.

The Lord, however, told Balaam under no circumstance was he to go with them to the Israelite camp. Balaam obeyed and sent Balak's escort away.

The temptation for money, however, was too great, and Balaam asked for God's permission. This time God relented and allowed him to go, but commanded Balaam to only speak the words He gave him.

The next day Balaam set off on his donkey. On the way the donkey moved off the road into a field. Next the donkey rubbed against a rock wall crushing Balaam's foot. Both times Balaam beat the donkey. Finally the donkey just sat down in the middle of the road refusing to go any further. When Balaam started to unmercifully beat the donkey the animal spoke.

"Why are you beating me?" the donkey said. "Have I ever done anything like this before?"

"No," Balaam replied, ignoring the realization he was speaking to a donkey.

Then the Angel of the Lord appeared to Balaam and said if it hadn't been for the donkey he'd be dead, because his way was against God. God used a talking donkey as a speed bump to slow his roll, and in the process bless Israel.

Humility is often referred to as the greatest virtue a man or woman of God can possess, which is the opposite of pride. It means to bring down, to have an attitude of lowliness, but it doesn't mean to be low.

It simply means having a right understanding of the human condition as sinners in direct comparison to a holy and righteous God.

The Lord installs speed bumps of humility to make sure we don't think more highly of ourselves than we ought to, like we're all that plus a bag of chips.

The Apostle Paul probably had this in mind when he said in Romans 12:3, "For I say, through the grace given to me, to everyone who is among you, not to think of himself more highly than he ought to think."

The Apostle Paul said, "Do nothing out of selfish ambition or vain conceit, but in humility consider others better than yourselves." (Philippians 2:3 NIV)

As we proceed to spiritual transformation where our goal is to be more like Jesus Christ, Jesus is the One we want to follow, both in His life and teachings.

We see this lived out at the Last Supper when Jesus washed the disciples' feet, even the feet of Judas Iscariot whom He knew would betray Him. Jesus took upon Himself the lowest position of a household slave.

Jesus said, "If I then, your Lord and Teacher, have washed your feet, you also ought to wash one another's feet. For I have given you an example that you should do as I have done to you." (John 13:14-15)

Jesus also taught this throughout His ministry.

"Unless you change and become like little children, you will never enter the kingdom of heaven. Therefore, whoever humbles himself like this child is the greatest in the kingdom of heaven." (Matthew 18:3-4 NIV)

Jesus is saying you'll be heaven ready and heaven bound when you humble yourself and become child-like in your faith.

Jesus also started His beatitudes with this value of humility, because humility is the key, not only to the kingdom of heaven but also to the rest of the beatitudes.

"Blessed are the poor in spirit, for theirs is the kingdom of heaven." (Matthew 5:3)

To be poor in spirit is to acknowledge our spiritual poverty because we cannot fill what's already full. We can't be filled until we're emptied.

Finally, the Lord considers and agrees to dwell with only those who are humble.

"I dwell in the high and holy place, with him who has a contrite and humble spirit, to revive the spirit of the humble, and to revive the heart of the contrite ones." (Isaiah 57:15)

Humility is an effective speed bump God uses to transform you and slow your roll so you can rightly understand who you are in the light of who God is.

Trials

One of the ways the Lord humbles us is by taking us through times of trials. It was with such humility that Jesus came.

In Philippians 2:8 the Apostle Paul said, "He humbled Himself and became obedient to the point of death, even the death of the cross."

Jesus definitely gives sufficient warning when it comes to this speed bump in our lives.

"In the world you will have tribulation; but be of good cheer, I have overcome the world," Jesus said in John 16:33.

These speed bumps come in the form of hard times, like divorce, unemployment, foreclosure, bankruptcy, crime, tragedies, accidents, and trauma of various sorts like sickness, disease, death, disappointments, and even loneliness.

Death being a speed bump might send some people over the edge saying, "This is going too far, and if this is the case, then this is not the God I want to follow."

But death is the natural outcome of life.

How can death, especially of a loved one, be transformational? How can it be looked on as a positive?

Solomon said in Ecclesiastes 7:2, "Better to go to the house of mourning than to go to the house of feasting, for that is the end of all men, and the living will take it to heart."

It's through death that we'll be better able to assess our mortality, and what we're doing in life that's going to count for eternity.

But trials don't have to stop us. Instead God uses them to slow us down, so don't look at them as liabilities we have to suffer through, but as opportunities from which we can grow.

The Apostle James said we should embrace such trials because they produce patience and a better ending.

"My brethren, count it all joy when you fall into various trials, knowing that the testing of your faith produces patience. But let patience have its perfect work, that you may be perfect and complete, lacking nothing." (James 1:2-4)

The Apostle Paul adds his two-cents, which is considerably more valuable than two-cents.

"And not only that, but we also glory in tribulations, knowing that tribulation produces perseverance, and perseverance, character, and character, hope." (Romans 5:3-5)

There are a slew of positive virtues acted upon through times of trial.

But the Apostle who really speaks to trials as a speed bump in our spiritual transformation is Peter.

"In this you greatly rejoice, though now for a little while, if need be, you have been grieved by various trials, that the genuineness of your faith, being much more precious than gold that perishes, though it is tested by fire, may be found to praise, honor, and glory at the revelation of Jesus Christ." (1 Peter 1:6-7)

Refining gold isn't simple. It is a very time-consuming process requiring a lot of heat. Our faith like gold needs to be refined as well, which takes not only time but also the heat of affliction.

God uses trials to bring us closer to Him, because there's no way we can do this, live life and go through trials, on our own. And while trials are hard, God didn't place them in our path to destroy us, but to make us stronger.

Fire doesn't hurt gold, only purifies it. In the same way, trials aren't meant to harm us, they're meant to refine, purify, and to test our faith and devotion to God. They reveal if we truly love God above everything and everyone else.

Further, whatever trials we go through, they won't last forever. Through them, however, we gain so much more.

The Apostle Paul said, "For our light and momentary troubles are achieving for us an eternal glory that far outweighs them all." (Corinthians 4:17 NIV)

No matter how light and momentary these trials may be, even though at the time they seem beyond comprehension, like they'll never end, remember that God hasn't placed them to destroy or stop our journey toward Him. Instead He placed them to slow us down so we'll take a serious look at the way we're going and to return to Him.

Suffering

People avoid pain and suffering at all costs. In fact, many within Christianity see suffering as coming from the pit of hell instead of the throne of heaven. A quick study in Job 1, however, reveals otherwise.

Here the Lord gives Satan the ability to attack, harass, and bring both physical and emotional suffering upon Job to reveal the genuineness of his faith.

For myself I know that what I suffered in losing everything wasn't Satan, rather it was the Lord allowing it to happen. He not only allowed it, He gave me the warning signs it was coming.

"What they meant for evil, I have meant it for good, in order to bring about the salvation of many." (Genesis 20:50 paraphrased)

God showed me He would restore what was taken, what the locust had eaten, His great army He sent against me, Joel 2:25-26.

God allowed the speed bump of suffering to get my attention and get me upon the path He had chosen, and in the process helped my faith grow. As the adage says, "No pain, no gain."

The Bible warns us not to let the speed bump of suffering catch us off guard, as if it was something strange happening. Instead it says to get ready.

"Beloved, do not think it strange concerning the fiery trial which is to try you, as though some strange thing happened to you." (1 Peter 4:12)

Probably the greatest example of suffering being a speed bump is the experience of Apostle Paul and the Lord's revelation about it. The exact nature of his suffering is unknown. We know only that three times he asked God to take it away.

"He (the Lord) said to me, 'My grace is sufficient for you, for My strength is made perfect in weakness.' Therefore most gladly I will rather boast in my infirmities, that the power of Christ may rest upon me." (2 Corinthians 12:9)

Paul went on to say he glories in his suffering for Christ's sake because through his weaknesses he's made strong through the power of the Lord.

Suffering is a direct result of the human condition brought upon the human race in the beginning. The condition we call sin. Suffering then shouldn't take us by surprise; it's a part of life.

It's in these times of suffering we become recipients of God's resources, most notably His grace and strength. Further, the sufferings bring us back to God and His word so we can live this life on purpose.

The Psalmist appreciated the things he suffered.

"Before I was afflicted I went astray, but now I keep Your word ... It is good for me that I have been afflicted, that I may learn Your statutes." (Psalm 119:67, 71)

Conclusion

Speed bumps are God's way of slowing our roll. The question becomes how can we slow down so these speed bumps don't violently jar loose our spiritual senses?

The answer? Prayer!

Through time in prayer we'll examine and reflect on God's Word, His ways, and where we're headed. The race to heaven isn't to the swift but to the slow.

At first we may not recognize or acknowledge these speed bumps are positive. We'll likely rebel against any thought that God would allow such things to happen. If we allow God's grace and mercy to take over, however, we'll see these speed bumps as something God puts together for our good.

As the Apostle Paul said in Romans 8:28, "And we know that all things work together for good to those who love God, to those who are the called according to His purpose."

Take a moment and think, look at those things we considered setbacks and how they turned out to be the very thing that helped us move forward on our journey of spiritual transformation; this journey of faith we're on.

Speed kills, especially when it comes to our spiritual transformation. Allow God's speed bumps to slow our roll. Take time to reflect on God's Word and the place the Lord may be leading.

When we encounter one of these speed bumps, we should keep our eyes focused on Jesus who not only is the way the truth and the life, John 14:6, but also the author and finisher of our faith, Hebrews 12:2.

So keep looking onto Jesus and let Him get us over the humps and speed bumps of life.

Reflection and Discussion

1. What sort of speed bumps has God set in your path? What were the lessons and what did you learn? How have they helped transform you spiritually?

2. Is there anything that you would consider beneath you like cleaning someone else's toilet? Why?

3. What have been the trials you've gone through? How did these help mold and shape your life?

4. The Psalmist better understood God's Word through the things he suffered. How has your understanding of God's Word increased through what you've suffered?

5. How has God's strength been magnified in your life through the trials and sufferings you've gone through?

6. What one thing will you take away from this chapter and apply to your life?

Chapter Fourteen

Maintaining Your Gains

We've reached the end of our journey toward spiritual transformation. Hopefully everyone has been following the advice by putting these various teachings into practice.

- Make sure you're on the right road, the narrow road through the narrow gate.

- Know who you are as a believer in Christ.

- Remember the soul scrubbing and heart cleansing measures of confession, forgiveness, and repentance.

- Get spiritually aligned with God, His word, His will, and His way.

- Become filled and baptized in the Holy Spirit.

- Activate the major agents of change; prophesy, prayer, and praise.

- Surrender and submit to the Lord.

- Learn how to be and stay on-purpose.

- Pursue the presence of God.

Maintaining Your Gains

- Avoid Satan's potholes, and slow down for God's speed bumps.

Maintaining gains we've achieved is popular in diet plans. Once we've reached our desired weight, we're encouraged to start a maintenance program. The same can be said about cars.

We're living in a day where everything is designed not only to break down, but also to break us down. When I turned my car in, the dealer said there wasn't much time left. He said cars were built to last only so many miles, although I don't remember that being said when he sold it to me. With every new vehicle there's a maintenance program that should be followed to extend the vehicle's life and keep the warranty active.

The importance of proper car maintenance is no secret. Either we maintain our cars in proper working order, or we'll find them dead on the side of the road at the most inconvenient times.

In order to help ensure this doesn't happen, the car's maker provides an instruction manual. Inside the manual there's a section on how to maintain the car. This maintenance manual provides a schedule of when the vehicle needs to be serviced to optimize its performance and longevity, not to mention keeping down costly repairs and tow charges. It provides time and mileage charts when the oil, filters, belts, and liquids need to be changed. The instruction manual has a list of everything that needs to be maintained and we would be wise to heed its instructions if we don't want to call a towing service.

Also, the older the car gets the more maintenance is required. It's safe to say this applies to our bodies as well. The older we become the more our bodies have to be maintained. This is also true of our spiritual lives. The longer we're on this journey, the more attacks come our way, the more potholes and speed bumps we'll hit. This calls for regular maintenance on our part.

Maintenance is the key if we want to remain on the straight and narrow road, and not find ourselves off in some ditch or stuck in a rut. As discussed earlier, the instruction manual for our spiritual transformation is God's Word. The Bible tells us not only how to maintain our relationship with God, but also how we are to maintain the gains we've made.

Let's discuss how to maintain our gains with God.

Put on God's armor

In Ephesians 6:11 the Apostle Paul said, "Put on the whole armor of God, that you may be able to stand against the wiles of the devil."

Our journey is not only lived out in the physical, but it's also spiritual. Therefore, to maintain our course and direction we need to understand we're going to run into opposition, spiritual opposition.

This is what the Apostle Paul meant when he said, "wiles of the devil." Wiles literally means the methodology or strategy Satan uses, which includes lies and deceit. It's Satan's plan of attack.

It comes in the form of people, businesses, organizations, institutions, governments, and even religions. Our fight isn't directly against them, nor is it against people, but rather it's against the spiritual powers behind them, or Satan.

"For we are not fighting against people made of flesh and blood, but against the evil rulers and authorities of the unseen world, against those mighty powers of darkness who rule this world, and against wicked spirits in the heavenly realms." (Ephesians 6:12 NLT)

Reading this may give us pause because of what's lined up against us. But all is not lost. There's good news. In this spiritual battle we've got the advantage, we've got the upper hand, because not only is the Holy Spirit in us greater than the devil and all his forces combined,1 John 4:4, but also once we are in Christ, the enemy cannot kill us spiritually. Our lives are hidden in Christ, Colossians 3:1-7.

Also realize that since it's a spiritual battle, this armor is spiritual as well, which means it isn't ours but God's.

This is actually the armor the Lord wears.

"He saw that there was no man and wondered that there was no intercessor; therefore His own arm brought salvation for Him, and His own righteousness, it sustained Him. For He put on righteousness as a breastplate and a helmet of salvation on His head; He put on the garments of vengeance for clothing and was clad with zeal as a cloak." (Isaiah 59:16-17)

We're commanded to put this same armor on, which in Greek means to envelop or hide ourselves so we're not exposed to the enemy's attacks. Also saying it's the whole armor means it's complete, lacking nothing in its ability to protect.

Think of it like Achilles of mythology. He fell in battle, not because he wasn't skilled but because his mother didn't completely dip him in the river Styx. She held him by his heel when she dipped him in the river in the process of making him invulnerable. In battle, however, he was hit with an arrow in that very heel. A person's weakness today is called their Achilles Heel.

Take a moment and look at this armor God has graciously given to help us in this battle to maintain our gains.

The belt of truth

In Roman armor the belt not only holds the tunic, but also keeps the body armor in place including the breastplate and the sword.

There's only one truth, God's. If there is another truth that contradicts the truth of God's Word, then it's not truth. There cannot be different truths.

The belt of truth is the truth of the revelation of God in Christ Jesus that sets us free, John 8:31-36; 43-45, and the truth we're supposed to walk in, that is, integrity and honesty, Psalm 51:6; Ephesians 4:15, 25. Anything other than this is the devil's territory.

So to put on the belt of truth is to live out the truth of God's Word.

The breastplate of righteousness

The purpose of the breastplate is to guard the body's most vital organs. Today we might call it a bulletproof vest.

As a breastplate of righteousness, what it means is that our righteousness doesn't come from ourselves. The prophet Isaiah aptly described this saying his righteousness before God was like filthy rags, Isaiah 64:6.

Therefore, the righteousness that counts is the righteousness that comes by faith in God. This was Abraham's testimony.

"He (Abraham) believed in the Lord and He (God) accounted it to him for righteousness." (Genesis 15:6)

Therefore, this breastplate of righteousness is the righteousness of God that comes through faith in Jesus Christ and what He did upon the cross. The breastplate of righteousness is our getting right with God through faith in Jesus' sacrifice for our sins.

The sandals of peace

The sandals were also called half boots worn by the Roman military. They were just as important as the rest of the armament. They were designed for the long marches over rough terrain that Roman soldiers were known for. The soles were studded with hobnails so the soldiers could stand firm against an enemy's attack.

Our sandals of peace and the firm foundation upon which we stand is the good news of Jesus Christ, the gospel message of salvation by grace through faith.

In John 14:27 Jesus said, "Peace I leave with you, My peace I give to you; not as the world gives do I give to you. Let not your heart be troubled, neither let it be afraid."

The gospel of Jesus Christ is the good news that we can have peace with God where before we were His enemy due to sin. The Apostle Paul said we were once alienated and an enemy of God. But through Jesus' death we've become reconciled back to God having peace with Him, Colossians 1:21-22.

Having received this good news of peace with God we can move forward with the same good news for others.

"How beautiful upon the mountains are the feet of him who brings good news, who proclaims peace, who brings glad tidings of good things, who proclaims salvation, who says to Zion, 'Your God reigns.'" (Isaiah 52:7)

If we want to succeed and be victorious on this journey, we not only have to be at peace with God, but share that peace with others.

The shield of faith

One of the deadliest weapons in Jesus' time was fiery darts. These darts were shorter than a spear but longer than an arrow. Their points were dipped in pitch and set on fire. These flaming darts would inflict serious damage on unprotected troops.

The Apostle Paul likens these darts to those temptations Satan continually launches against us. And the only thing that will stop and quench them is the shield of faith.

Roman soldiers had two different shields, one small and the other large, about 2 ½ feet wide by 4 ½ feet long. They were made with layered wood covered in hide and bound with iron. They were designed to keep the soldier safe against the enemy's fiery darts. The points would stick in the shield and be quenched by the leather that when possible was doused with water.

The shield of faith that quenches Satan's fiery darts of doubts, despair, discouragement, depression, and disillusionment is our faith in God. We are told to walk by faith and not by sight, which is apropos because we'll never see these fiery darts coming until after they hit.

Our faith is to be in God and His promises, like the promise that He'll never leave or forsake us, Hebrews 13:5. Our trust in God's promises as our shield is Solomon's point.

"Every word of God is pure; He is a shield to those who put their trust in Him." (Proverbs 30:5)

The helmet of salvation

No soldier in his right mind (pun intended) would go into battle without his helmet. It would protect his head from the enemy's arrows and glancing sword blows. It covered the whole head, leaving the face or just the eyes exposed.

Paul states the helmet is a Christian's knowledge of their salvation, which protects their thought life. One of Satan's tactics is to attack our thought life, especially when it comes to our salvation. He loves to accuse us saying we're not worthy of salvation, and how can we be saved when we do such awful things. Satan also wants us to doubt God's goodness, God's ability to forgive us, and the truthfulness of His word.

The knowledge we've been saved by faith helps keep doubts at bay. With this knowledge we can defeat the enemy, because there is no condemnation to those who are in Christ Jesus, Romans 8:1. With the helmet of salvation firmly in place we can have confidence moving forward knowing that nothing can separate us from the love of God, Romans 8:35, 38-39.

So a mind covered with the helmet of salvation is a mind controlled by God and His word, rather than a mind controlled by this world, which so happens to be controlled by Satan.

The sword of the spirit

Up to this point we've looked at weapons that are defensive in nature that protect us from the forces of evil. But we're not to stay on the defensive, rather we are to stand and move against evil. Jesus said that when we do, the gates of Hell wouldn't be able to prevail against us.

The sword of the spirit, which Paul identifies as the Word of God, is offensive in nature (again pun intended).

"For the word of God is living and powerful and sharper than any two-edged sword, piercing even to the division of soul and spirit and of joints and marrow, and is a discerner of the thoughts and intents of the heart." (Hebrews 4:12)

But while it's a weapon of offense, it is also a defensive weapon as well, parrying the enemy's thrusts against us. This is seen in Satan's attacks on Jesus in the wilderness. Three times He tempted Jesus, and three times Jesus parried the attacks saying; "It is written."

The Apostle Paul says all Scripture is God breathed, 2 Timothy 3:16, that is, the Holy Spirit inspires it. It is the Holy Spirit who helps us wield it, but to wield it we have to know it.

There is one more offensive weapon in a believer's arsenal.

Praying in the Spirit

Praying in the Spirit has been debated in the church, but let me give you an all-inclusive answer. Its prayer directed and inspired by the Holy Spirit.

In Romans 8:26 the Apostle Paul said, "Likewise the Spirit also helps in our weaknesses. For we do not know what we should pray for as we ought, but the Spirit himself makes intercession for us with groanings that cannot be uttered."

Praying in the Spirit is our long-range artillery. It pounds the enemy's position and weakens his attacks, because the Holy Spirit knows exactly where to aim to do the most damage.

The Apostle Paul's advice is to pray always with all the prayer we can muster and make sure it's fueled and directed by the Holy Spirit.

Practice the disciplines

We dealt with this in the chapter "Agents of Change," and the three greatest agents of change are prophecy, prayer, and praise. While these are the greatest disciplines for spiritual transformation, there are also other disciplines to help maintain our gains.

To his protégé Timothy the Apostle Paul said, "Train yourself to be godly. For physical training is of some value, but godliness has value for all things, holding promise for both the present life and the life to come." (1 Timothy 4:7b-8 NIV)

Take daily time in reading and hearing God's Word, along with praying and praising the Lord. But there are many other disciplines as well that help maintain our spiritual life and help keep us on this road to heaven.

These include the disciplines of serving, stewardship, submission, silence, solitude, evangelism, fasting, journaling, meditation, and fellowship.

By faith celebrate

Most Christians take themselves and this journey way too seriously, forgetting their salvation is a time for great joy, not sorrow, which is how many Christians look when they're in church, that is, they look like they've sucked on one too many lemons.

Being a Christian isn't about doom and gloom, rather it's a life filled with joy.

In John 15:11 Jesus said, "These things I have spoken to you, that My joy may remain in you, and that your joy may be full."

Solomon said there's a time for everything. He said there is a time to weep and mourn; there is a time to laugh and dance, Ecclesiastes 3:4.

Solomon added that a merry heart is good medicine, because it brings great cheer to your face, or better yet your attitude, Proverbs 17:22; 15:13.

Joy is an important component on this journey of faith, because it gives you strength to carry on.

"Do not sorrow, for the joy of the Lord is your strength." (Nehemiah 8:10a)

We need to celebrate with joy the gains we've made on this journey of faith, because if we don't do a little celebrating, then sooner rather than later we'll move toward trying to find ways outside the Lord to find happiness.

Joy isn't in the circumstances you face in life, nor can joy be manufactured through rah-rah meetings. Your joy is found only in the Lord and it is in the Lord we rejoice.

"Rejoice in the Lord always. Again I will say, rejoice!" (Philippians 4:4)

You need to make some noise and by faith celebrate what Jesus has done in your life, bringing you into a right relationship with God and into an eternity in heaven where there will be no more tears of sorrow but only of unspeakable joy in the presence of God.

Now that's something to get excited about, something to rejoice in, and something to celebrate.

Conclusion

We've finished our study toward spiritual transformation. I pray that we understand the importance of these transformational steps and stay connected to our ultimate guide, the Holy Spirit, Who will lead us not only in the way of truth, but also in the will of God.

Reflection and Discussion

1. In what practical ways can you put on God's defensive armor?

    a. The belt of truth?

    b. The breastplate of righteousness?

    c. The sandals of peace?

    d. The shield of faith?

    e. The helmet of salvation?

2. In what practical ways can we use God's offensive weapons?

    a. The sword of the spirit?

    b. Praying in the Spirit?

3. How can you begin joyfully celebrating your salvation and the gains you've made as a Christian?

4. What one thing will you take away from this chapter and apply to your life?

About the Author

Dennis Lee is a past business owner who operated a multi-million dollar office supply and equipment company along with several small businesses in Las Vegas, Nevada.

He graduated from the University of Nevada Las Vegas with a Bachelors in Business Administration, a Masters of Arts in Theology from Talbot School of Theology, along with a Masters of Divinity equivalency degree from Fuller Theological Seminary.

After graduation from Talbot in 1995 Dennis took over as senior pastor of Hallelujah Christian Fellowship, a non-denominational church in Las Vegas, Nevada. After 10 years he moved to Mesquite, Nevada, where he is presently the senior pastor of Living Waters Fellowship, a Foursquare church.

Dennis is a prolific writer, writing two weekly columns in the Desert Valley Times, "Lessons in Leadership," and "Rediscover the Bible for Life." He also writes daily devotionals that he post on Facebook.

"I've had the pleasure of knowing Dennis Lee for the past four years. Dennis is gifted, diligent and courageous. As a pastor, he is committed to reaching and impacting his community and looks for opportunities to do so. He loves the Word of God and realizes how valuable it is in order to see true transformation take place. In working with Dennis, I've discovered a person who has strong ideas and beliefs, yet has humility and is teachable. As a writer, he is a gifted communicator and uses this gift to help people discover how great God is and how they can walk in His plan. I gladly endorse Pastor Dennis!"

- Kimberly Dirmann,
Southwest District Supervisor,
The Foursquare Church

"For the last 14 years I have served as Senior Pastor at First Baptist Church of Mesquite. I have had the privilege of knowing and working with Dennis as a fellow laborer in Christ. Dennis has stood by the pastors of our community with wisdom and support. His writing in the local paper has touched many lives. He continues to encourage and be there for anyone who is struggling and has been there for me through the trials of ministry.

- Bill Stevenson,
Senior Pastor,
First Baptist Church in Mesquite, NV.

CPSIA information can be obtained
at www.ICGtesting.com
Printed in the USA
BVHW080907080719
552754BV00008B/135/P